IBM Watson Projects

Eight exciting projects that put artificial intelligence into
practice for optimal business performance

James Miller

BIRMINGHAM - MUMBAI

IBM Watson Projects

Commissioning Editor: Pravin Dhandre
Acquisition Editor: Tushar Gupta
Content Development Editor: Snehal Kolte
Technical Editor: Dharmendra Yadav
Copy Editor: Safis Editing
Project Coordinator: Manthan Patel
Proofreader: Safis Editing
Indexer: Pratik Shirodkar
Graphics: Jisha Chirayil
Production Coordinator: Arvindkumar Gupta

First published: September 2018

Production reference: 1290918

Published by Packt Publishing Ltd.
Livery Place
35 Livery Street
Birmingham
B3 2PB, UK.

ISBN 978-1-78934-371-7

www.packtpub.com

`mapt.io`

Mapt is an online digital library that gives you full access to over 5,000 books and videos, as well as industry leading tools to help you plan your personal development and advance your career. For more information, please visit our website.

Why subscribe?

- Spend less time learning and more time coding with practical eBooks and Videos from over 4,000 industry professionals

- Improve your learning with Skill Plans built especially for you

- Get a free eBook or video every month

- Mapt is fully searchable

- Copy and paste, print, and bookmark content

Packt.com

Did you know that Packt offers eBook versions of every book published, with PDF and ePub files available? You can upgrade to the eBook version at `www.packt.com` and as a print book customer, you are entitled to a discount on the eBook copy. Get in touch with us at `customercare@packtpub.com` for more details.

At `www.packt.com`, you can also read a collection of free technical articles, sign up for a range of free newsletters, and receive exclusive discounts and offers on Packt books and eBooks.

Contributors

About the author

James Miller is an innovator and accomplished Sr. Project Lead and Solution Architect with 37 years experience. of extensive design and development across multiple platforms and technologies. Roles include leveraging his consulting experience to provide hands-on leadership in all phases of advanced analytics and related technology projects, providing recommendations for process improvement, report accuracy, adoption of disruptive technologies, enablement, and insight identification.
Author: *Statistics for Data Science, Mastering Predictive Analytics w/R, Big Data Visualization, Learning Watson Analytics, Implementing Splunk, Mastering Splunk, 5 Guiding Principles of a Successful Center of Excellence*, and *TM1 Developer's Certification Guide*.

This book is dedicated to my wife Nanette and my children Shelby and Paige - Love Always

About the reviewer

Mayur Ravindra Narkhede has a good blend of experience in data science and industrial domain. He is a researcher with a B.Tech in computer science and an M.Tech in CSE with a specialization in Artificial Intelligence.

A data scientist whose core experience lies in building automated end-to-end solutions, he is proficient at applying technology, AI, ML, data mining, and design thinking to better understand and predict improvements in business functions and desirable requirements with growth profitability.

He has worked on multiple advanced solutions, such as ML and predictive model development for the oil and gas industry, financial services, road traffic and transport, life sciences, and the big data platform for asset-intensive industries.

Packt is searching for authors like you

If you're interested in becoming an author for Packt, please visit `authors.packtpub.com` and apply today. We have worked with thousands of developers and tech professionals, just like you, to help them share their insight with the global tech community. You can make a general application, apply for a specific hot topic that we are recruiting an author for, or submit your own idea.

Table of Contents

Preface

IBM Watson provides fast, intelligent insight in ways that the human brain simply can't match. Through eight different projects, this book helps you to explore the computing and analytical capabilities of IBM Watson.

The book begins by refreshing your knowledge of IBM Watson's basic data preparation capabilities, such as adding and exploring data to prepare it for being applied to models. The projects covered in this book can be developed for different industries, such as banking, healthcare, the media, and security. These projects will enable you to develop an AI mindset and guide you in developing smart data-driven projects, including automating supply chains, analyzing sentiment in social media datasets, and developing personalized recommendations.

By the end of this book, you'll have learned how to develop solutions for process automation, and you'll be able to make better data-driven decisions to deliver an excellent customer experience.

Who this book is for

This book is for data scientists, AI engineers, NLP engineers, machine learning engineers, and data analysts who wish to build next-generation analytics applications. Basic familiarity with cognitive computing and sound knowledge of any programming language is all you need to understand the projects covered in this book.

What this book covers

Chapter 1, *The Essentials of IBM Watson*, defines the latest version of (IBM) Watson Analytics and outlines various uses of the tool. In addition, the chapter provides an overview of Watson's interface and its major components, as well as offering a refresher on basic tasks such as adding data, exploring data, and creating a prediction.

Chapter 2, *A Basic Watson Project*, analyzes trip logs from a driving services company to determine which trip characteristics have a direct effect on a trip's profitability, what type of trip is most profitable, and which are prone to complications. This first project serves to cover the basics of a simple Watson project, preparing the reader for the upcoming, more complex projects presented in the following chapters.

Chapter 3, *An Automated Supply Chain Scenario*, consists of a use case project that focuses on analyzing how effective a supply chain is for a retail department store. This automated supply chain scenario provides insights into an organization's supply chain data and processes, in an attempt to isolate the cause of poor delivery performance.

Chapter 4, *Healthcare Dialoguing*, analyzes Watson's cognitive assistance solution, specifically with regard to creating an engaging dialog between healthcare providers and their patients. This project establishes relevant recommendations based upon patient inputs.

Chapter 5, *Social Media Sentiment Analysis*, tackles sentimental analysis using Watson to automatically analyze and categorize text posted to social media in an attempt to determine an audience's feeling about a topic.

Chapter 6, *Pattern Recognition and Classification*, discusses pattern recognition and using Watson to identify regularities in data in an effort to automatically classify athletes positionally based upon data provided.

Chapter 7, *Retail and Personalized Recommendations*, introduces the concept of personalized recommendations and the use of Watson to create a specialized plan through conversion. In this project, the objective is to create an individualized plan based upon characteristics found within a pool of data.

Chapter 8, *Integration for Sales Forecasting*, discusses integrating Watson with an organization's forecasting system in order to test its product sales forecasting effectiveness, comparing forecasts to actual results.

Chapter 9, *Anomaly Detection in Banking with AI*, uses Artificial Intelligence (AI) from a Watson perspective, walking through an example use case project related to the banking industry, in which transactions are evaluated to identify fraud.

Chapter 10, *What's Next?*, summarizes what readers have learned in the preceding chapters and what they can do next to continue the Watson learning process.

To get the most out of this book

Basic familiarity with cognitive computing and sound knowledge of any programming language is all you need to understand the projects covered in this book.

Download the example code files

You can download the example code files for this book from your account at
`www.packt.com`. If you purchased this book elsewhere, you can visit
`www.packt.com/support` and register to have the files emailed directly to you.

You can download the code files by following these steps:

1. Log in or register at `www.packt.com`.
2. Select the **SUPPORT** tab.
3. Click on **Code Downloads & Errata**.
4. Enter the name of the book in the **Search** box and follow the onscreen
   instructions.

Once the file is downloaded, please make sure that you unzip or extract the folder using the
latest version of:

- WinRAR/7-Zip for Windows
- Zipeg/iZip/UnRarX for Mac
- 7-Zip/PeaZip for Linux

The code bundle for the book is also hosted on GitHub at `https://github.com/
PacktPublishing/IBM-Watson-Project`. In case there's an update to the code, it will be
updated on the existing GitHub repository.

We also have other code bundles from our rich catalog of books and videos available
at `https://github.com/PacktPublishing/`. Check them out!

Conventions used

There are a number of text conventions used throughout this book.

`CodeInText`: Indicates code words in text, database table names, folder names, filenames,
file extensions, pathnames, dummy URLs, user input, and Twitter handles. Here is an
example: "we can locate and select our `SuperSupplyChain` file."

Bold: Indicates a new term, an important word, or words that you see on screen. For
example, words in menus or dialog boxes appear in the text like this. Here is an example:
The information box shows that **Guide** is the strongest predictor of **TipGrade**.

Warnings or important notes appear like this.

 Tips and tricks appear like this.

Get in touch

Feedback from our readers is always welcome.

General feedback: If you have questions about any aspect of this book, mention the book title in the subject of your message and email us at customercare@packtpub.com.

Errata: Although we have taken every care to ensure the accuracy of our content, mistakes do happen. If you have found a mistake in this book, we would be grateful if you would report this to us. Please visit www.packt.com/submit-errata, selecting your book, clicking on the Errata Submission Form link, and entering the details.

Piracy: If you come across any illegal copies of our works in any form on the Internet, we would be grateful if you would provide us with the location address or website name. Please contact us at copyright@packt.com with a link to the material.

If you are interested in becoming an author: If there is a topic that you have expertise in and you are interested in either writing or contributing to a book, please visit authors.packtpub.com.

Reviews

Please leave a review. Once you have read and used this book, why not leave a review on the site that you purchased it from? Potential readers can then see and use your unbiased opinion to make purchase decisions, we at Packt can understand what you think about our products, and our authors can see your feedback on their book. Thank you!

For more information about Packt, please visit packt.com.

The Essentials of IBM Watson 1

IBM Watson Analytics brings smart data analysis and visualization, guided data discovery, automated predictive analytics, and cognitive capabilities to you as a service.

Through the process of making a project, this book attempts to help developers and business users alike learn the various computing and analytical capabilities of IBM Watson Analytics.

This book looks at each and every capability of the IBM Watson Analytics platform, such as speeding up predictive analytics for better business insights, building tailored interactions for an improved customer experience, identifying trends, investigating potential issues, and so on, thereby allowing readers to start building projects in their business context using Watson Analytics.

By the end of this book, you should be ready to use Watson Analytics to make better data-driven decisions, as well as visualize and communicate any analysis of your data that you might gain using Watson Analytics.

In this first chapter, we will try to define the latest version of IBM Watson Analytics and look at the various objectives of the tool. In addition, this chapter will provide an overview of Watson's interface, as well its major components, to offer a refresher on some basic tasks, such as adding data, exploring data, and creating a prediction.

This chapter will cover the following topics:

- Definition and objectives
- Exploring the Watson interface
- A refresher of the basic tasks

Definition and objectives

Here's an interesting factoid—**IBM Watson** was named after IBM's first CEO and industrialist Thomas J. Watson (who has been credited with developing IBM's management style and corporate culture), and was specifically developed to answer questions on the quiz show Jeopardy!

IBM Watson has been described as a computer system that is based on **cognitive computing** and that, conceptually, can deliver answers to your questions.

Now the term *cognitive* also has an interesting definition. It is defined as being concerned with the act or process of knowing, or perceiving, which, as you can imagine, is enormously valuable to any business.

Cognitive algorithms have the ability to create insights and make evidence-based decisions in ambiguous circumstances, based upon as much data as possible.

 IBM Watson is the AI platform for professionals. Watson gives your business distinct advantages. Beyond optimizing the tasks that you already do, AI enables new ways of doing business. Find out more at the Watson website at: https://www.ibm.com/watson/about.

IBM Watson is exciting because it attempts (in much the same way as a human would) to review the provided raw data and reason out an answer. In fact, Watson yields more of a hypothesis than an answer (based upon both the data and other dependencies or circumstances).

The concept of answering with a best-suited answer rather than simply providing a calculated response is an important mind shift that opens organizations up to processing all types and formats of data to produce new and valuable insights as a return on their data investment. These insights aren't typically exposed by using only mainstream, noncognitive approaches.

Another Watson plus is that while consuming data, Watson converts unstructured data into structured data, which then allows that data to be available for those traditional downstream, noncognitive, more mainstream analytical and reporting tools and solutions.

The techniques applied by IBM Watson allow the possibility of using not just the original questions but also subsequent questions to find the right answers, possibly inferred by assembling multiple fragments of raw data and artifacts from multiple sources via machine learning algorithms. Watson provides this expertise to everyone, with the goal of addressing an entirely new class of problems and solutions that will fundamentally change the relationship of people, business, and computers.

This is the objective of IBM Watson, and is most likely one of the objectives of you, the reader of this book.

With any luck, as you work through the following chapters and gain a level of comfort in using IBM Watson Analytics, you will begin to think about and approach problems and opportunities in a new way.

In the following sections of this chapter, we will review the fundamentals of the IBM Watson interface, as well as some of the basic tasks you'll need to be familiar with in order to successfully work through the case study examples given in the following chapters.

Let's go!

IBM Cloud prerequisites

IBM Watson lives in the cloud (the IBM Cloud). The cloud environment makes it relatively easy to get started as there are actually very few prerequisites that you need to access IBM Watson Analytics (and the IBM Cloud platform overall). In fact, all you really need to get yourself up and running is an up-to-date web browser (most will work quite adequately) and your willingness to discover and learn.

The following are the official browser minimum requirements (as of the time of writing):

- **Chrome**: Latest version for your operating system
- **Firefox**: Latest regular and ESR versions for your operating system
- **Internet Explorer**: Version 11
- **Edge**: Latest version for Windows
- **Safari**: Latest version for Mac

Exploring the Watson interface

With any new endeavor, one would be wise to take some time before actually bringing or attempting any project work (so, at the startup stage) in order to focus on becoming comfortable, or at least somewhat familiar, with the tool or technology's fundamentals.

In this chapter, as we look at IBM Watson, obtaining this understanding starts first with procuring access to IBM Watson Analytics and, as a next step, the **IBM Cloud platform**.

First, a little bit on the IBM Cloud. The IBM Cloud is a platform offering a rich assortment of infrastructure, cognitive, software, and services (and a *lot* of documentation and examples) with the aim of jump starting and otherwise accelerating the pace of business.

The IBM Cloud platform is where you can access the full power of the IBM Watson platform, where you can build new and exciting applications, using prebuilt services and APIs.

At the time of writing, to access the IBM Cloud platform, you can go to: `https://console.bluemix.net` to log in or create an account.

Once you obtain your access, you will have the opportunity to click through a number of welcome, how-to, and helpful hint tutorials. The introductory window is shown in the following screenshot:

The reader should take note that the official product documentation refers to the IBM Cloud user interface as the Cloud Console, where all of your cloud resources, as well as components (including IBM Watson), can be accessed and managed.

After you log in, your dashboard will contain many links to various resources and functionalities based upon your account type. The following screenshot shows the IBM Cloud main or start page (sometimes even called the **welcome page**), which is referred to as the IBM Cloud **Dashboard**:

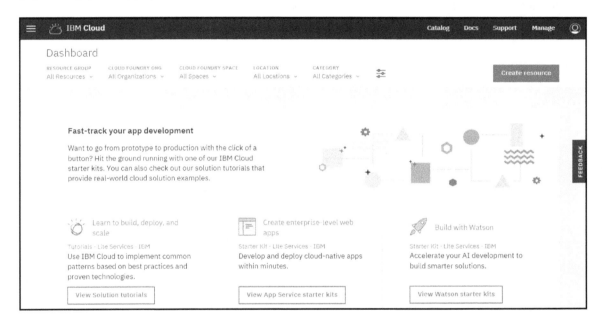

We won't take the time here to go through these wonderful IBM Cloud platform tutorial videos (but you definitely should review as many of them as possible); instead, we will talk a bit about the basic components of the IBM Cloud Console and then quickly-jump into the IBM Watson Analytics interface.

The menu bar

The menu bar (located across the top of the dashboard) is sometimes referred to as the title bar. The following is a screenshot showing the IBM Cloud menu bar:

In the following sections, we will look at the icons and options in the menu bar, starting from the top left side.

Menu icon

The menu icon is the first image on the left of the menu bar (Hint: it looks like a stack of three lines). Clicking on this icon will display a vertical list of the available menu selections on the platform. The following screenshot shows the menu selection list:

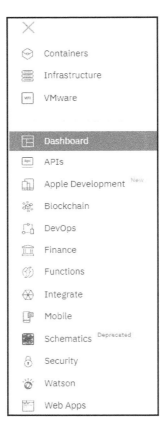

 A very helpful feature that IBM Cloud provides is the highlighted status indicators next to certain listed selections. For example, **New** and **Deprecated** are shown in the preceding screenshot, and they alert the user to menu selections that have been recently added or are scheduled for removal (also know as deprecated).

IBM Cloud

As we move to the right along the title bar, the next option is the **IBM Cloud**
menu selection. Clicking on this option will always return you—send you back—to the
start or main page.

Catalog

The **Catalog** menu selection sends you to the **Catalog** IBM Cloud page (shown in the
following screenshot), where you can (based upon a selected filter type) do things such as
manage your cloud infrastructure and access other IBM Cloud platform features:

Docs

Clicking the **Docs** menu item takes you to the **Docs** or **Documentation Entry** page (shown in the following screenshot). Here is where you can perform actions such as **Search documentation**, **Get started by deploying your first app**, or follow a specific IBM Cloud help thread that you are interested in:

Support

Clicking on the **Support** menu item displays a drop-down selection list (shown in the following screenshot) with various options for obtaining the best type or level of support based upon your particular needs. The support options included are as follows:

- **What's New**
- Access to the (IBM Cloud) **Support Center**
- The ability to enter or **Add** (a) **Ticket** (a ticket is your request for information or support assistance)
- **View Tickets** (that is, all of your current and prior tickets)
- **Status**, where you have the ability to investigate issues reported by the entire IBM Cloud user community:

Manage

Clicking on the **Manage** menu option displays the various areas in which you have the ability to manage your IBM Cloud's **Account**, **Billing and Usage**, and **Security**:

Profile – avatar

Clicking on the **Profile** menu option displays access to view, update, and upgrade options for your IBM Cloud account. In addition, this is where you can officially log out of the IBM Cloud environment:

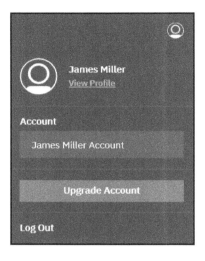

 It is a best practice recommendation to ALWAYS formally log out of your IBM Cloud account (rather than just closing your browser).

Online glossary, let's chat, and feedback

Another great resource for someone who is new to the IBM Cloud is the online glossary of terms, referred to as the **IBM Cloud Glossary**, which can be found at:

`https://console.bluemix.net/docs/overview/glossary/index.html#glossr`

In addition, on most pages within the IBM Cloud environment, you will see the following icon:

This is the Let's Chat icon which, by clicking, connects you within a few hours to a question and answer dialog with one or more IBM Cloud Support Experts. It is not a real-time chat session, but it is pretty efficient. Don't be afraid to give it a try, they are very helpful.

IBM is committed to growing and evolving the IBM Cloud platform and is keen on hearing your opinion. One testimonial to this commitment is the presence of the **FEEDBACK** label, which is visible on most of the pages within the IBM Cloud. Clicking on **FEEDBACK** presents you with the option to easily provide both specific or (more) general comments and suggestions, or, if you are having a problem, from here you can also enter a support ticket.

What about Watson?

Back to our menu icon. If you scroll down, you can click on **Watson**, which will send you to the IBM Watson main page, shown as follows:

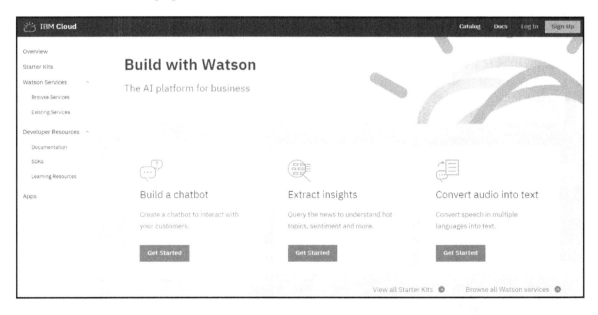

The format of this page is similar in format to the IBM Cloud console main page, as there are helpful **Get Started** panels (sometimes called **tiles**) offering options across the top part of the page. These are links to **Starter Kits**, and beneath these most popular kits (**Build a chatbot, Extract insights**, and **Convert audio into text**) are the links to **View all Starter Kits** and **Browse all Watson services**.

If you scroll further down the page, you will find access to **Watson Studio**, as well other useful links such as **SDKs**, The **Watson Blog**, **GitHub**, and so on.

 The links and panels/tiles that are displayed here will change from time to time based upon a variety of factors, so it is a good practice to take a few minutes periodically and review what is offered.

Accessing the **IBM Watson platform** through the IBM Cloud platform is the approach you will use for building advanced apps using Watson services, APIs, and SDKs, but you can use Watson Analytics for advanced projects by accessing the Watson Analytics interface directly.

You can find this Watson entry point at: `https://watson.analytics.ibmcloud.com` (and access it with your same valid IBM user ID).

The Watson dashboard

Like the IBM Cloud dashboard, the Watson dashboard is organized with a title or menu bar across the top of the page, (see following sections) which I call the quick start information bar. Beneath that, you'll find the **Search/Add/Filter/Sort bar**, followed by an open space where content panels will appear (more about these later, also know that these are sometimes called **tiles** or **informational titles**).

Let's review each of these areas, starting at the top.

Menu bar

The Watson Analytics menu bar shows the Watson name in the far left. In the center of the bar there is a drop-down list that allows you to quickly jump between open Watson pages. This is kind of such as clicking on **open applications** on your desktop:

For example, in the following example, we see **Welcome** and **our Bus Runs - Trip Issues** in the list. Clicking on either entry jumps to that view:

The logged in user name (the name of the logged in user) is always displayed to the right of the quick jump list. This is where you can manage your Watson Analytics account, perform Watson Administrative work, or log out:

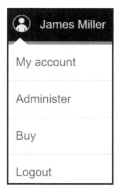

Next, on the menu bar, you'll find access to the product documentation, helpful hints that have been documented by IBM and the Watson user community, as well as access to the ever-growing (now including you!) Watson community.

Finally, on the far right of the Watson menu bar, there is the Collections icon, where one can access all Watson Assets that you have created as well as those that have been shared with you.

Quick start information bar

Under the Watson Analytics menu bar is the Quick Start Information bar. It consists of larger icons used to organize and provide quick access to selected functionalities. These functionalities currently include: **Explore**, **Predict**, **Assemble**, **Social Media**, and **Refine** (all of which we will use throughout the chapters of this book):

Search, add, filter, and sort

Here, you will find the features that allow you to (wildcard) search for, sort, and otherwise filter the content panels/tiles that currently exist within your Watson Analytics account.

In the center, perhaps most importantly, is the **Add** icon. This allows you to create new Watson assets or add more data to your Watson account. The following screenshot shows the **Search** bar:

Content panel area

And finally, all of the Watson Analytics assets you either previously created or have been granted access to will show up here as individual **content panels/tiles** that you can click on to access and edit/update:

PREDICTION	PREDICTION	DATA SET CSV	PREDICTION
our Bus Runs - Trip Issues	Bus Runs - Trip Issues	CombinedBusRuns	Runs
Dec 30, 2015	Dec 30, 2015	Dec 30, 2015	Dec 28, 2015

(51 MEDIUM QUALITY)

Now that we have gone through our quick interface investigation, let's go over some of the more basic (but absolutely critical) Watson tasks. Throughout the rest of the chapter, we'll review the areas of Watson that involve **Explore**, **Predict**, **Assemble**, **Social Media**, **Refine**, **Save**, and **Add** (ing data).

Basic tasks refresher

In this section, we will look into the basic tasks of IBM Watson.

The first step

Before you can do anything with Watson, you need to set up an account (and for general discovery, you can use the free version!) and log in. You can get started with IBM Watson by going directly to: `https://watson.analytics.ibmcloud.com` (as of this writing) and (or course!) using user your IBM ID to sign-in (or sign-up if you're a new user).

Not too much more to add here on this topic, as logging in is pretty much self-explanatory.

Explore

Typically, one would start by adding data—some project-focused new data—to IBM Watson, but for now, as we are just reviewing the basics of the Watson interface, we'll mention that IBM Watson offers a pretty extensive library of sample data, which is always available to you to use in your efforts to gain an understanding of how the basic functions and features of the tool work.

So, with those thoughts in mind we'll move right along, starting here with a discussion on **Explore**, which is, starting from left to right, the first IBM Watson feature available on the **start-up** bar.

IBM Watson **Explore** is designed to allow you to effortlessly integrate the use of visualizations in an effort to gain an understanding of the data you are interested in, so that you can notice patterns and relationships within that data. These can then have major impacts on the business or problem you are solving for.

Watson Analytics makes it easy to jump right in and get going with the process of data exploration without requiring a lot of setup or data preparation.

After clicking **Explore**, the **Create new exploration dialog** (shown in the following screenshot) offers you a list of existing datasets (if you've already added any to Watson) to begin exploring as well as the ability to **add your data** by browsing to a file or selecting Twitter as the data's **source**, and finally, you can also explore the **Sample data** offered by Watson:

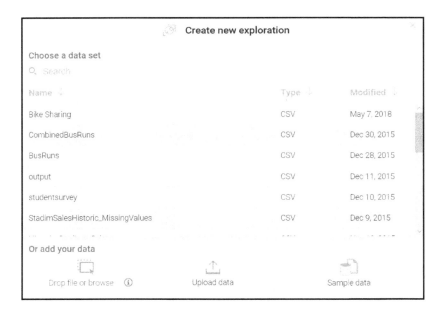

 As we go over the Watson start-ups, you will notice that they all employ sort of a standard dialog formatted very much the same; you have the ability to choose an existing starting point, add a new one, or just get started with sample data.

Watson prompts

What's exciting is what happens after you select a dataset. IBM Watson asks you: **What do you want to explore in your selected dataset?** and also prompts you with suggested **starting points** based on the data you selected.

In the following example, we have selected a dataset named **Bike Sharing**:

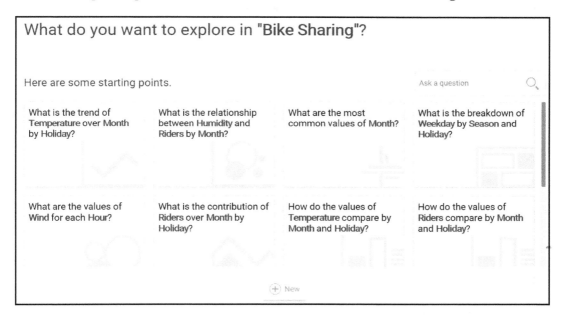

Predict

The IBM Watson **Predict** feature delivers highly interpretable insights that are based on internal Watson complex modeling. In the **Predict** capability, Watson Analytics uses sophisticated algorithms to quickly and efficiently deliver its predictions based on the data you provide.

Just like the previously-mentioned Explore capability, once you click on **Predict**, IBM Watson provides you with the **Create new prediction** dialog (shown in the following screenshot), which displays a list of existing datasets that you can select as the source for your new Watson prediction, as well as the option to upload/add new data (or utilize the provided sample data):

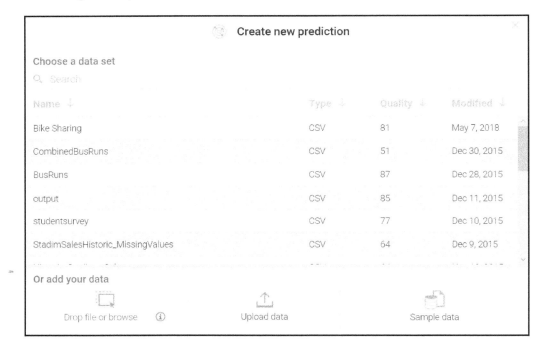

IBM Watson Predict automatically identifies the data that you are analyzing and includes *visual* as well as textual understandings that are generated from your selected data.

Watson couldn't make it much easier! The basic steps for using **Predict** are simply:

1. Add (or select) some data
2. Click **Predict** (to tell Watson to create the prediction)
3. View the results!

Creating your prediction (after selecting the data source) starts with the **Create a new Analysis** dialog (a bit of a misnomer; are we creating a new analysis or prediction?) where you provide a name and target:

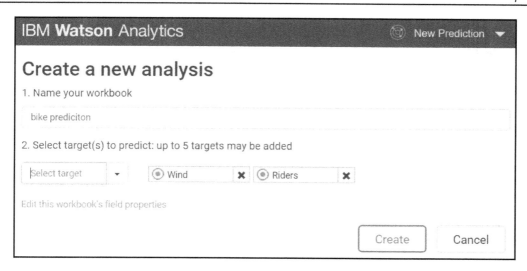

Next, you click **Create** and let Watson do its work:

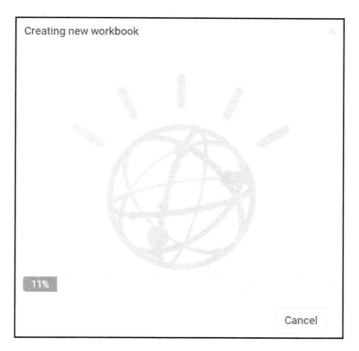

And then (momentarily), we have our prediction:

Top predictors of Riders

Assemble

Another fundamental feature of IBM Watson is **Assemble**. Simply put, you can use this to group the results generated from using **Explore** and **Predict**.

Clicking on **Assemble**, you will see a dialog with a familiar format:

Again, you have the option to **select an existing dataset** or **add your new data** (you also have another misnomer, **Create a new view** even though you clicked on **Assemble**). You also have the option of clicking on **Skip**, but for now, we see that the next page is where you do the assembling by entering a name and selecting a Watson template:

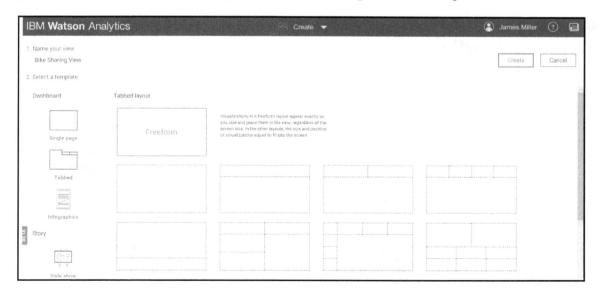

Selecting a Watson template

Once you select a template (templates are the way you can easily organize your artifacts) and click **Create** you can then build your **Assembly** (or view) by dragging and dropping various data points into your favorite visualizations (more on this later!):

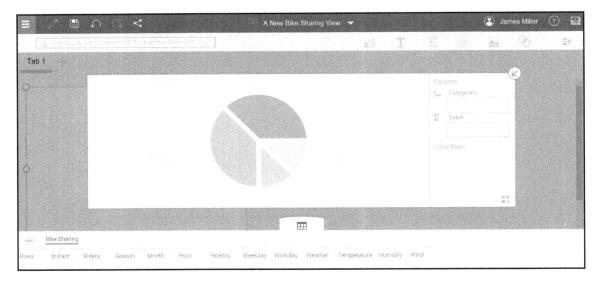

Building your Assembly

Social media

Newer to IBM Watson are the built-in Social Media capabilities. Now, you can discover insights based upon data gathered by IBM Watson from key words and hashtags you choose. This data can be from Twitter, forums, reviews, Facebook pages, video descriptions, comments, blogs, and other news sources. Exploring and analyzing social media trends is now a fundamental task using IBM Watson.

 Depending on your subscription level (version), the number and type of social media documents (such as Facebook pages) that you can retrieve may have different limits.

Clicking on **Social Media** presents the **Create a new social media project** dialog (shown as follows) that steps you through the process of creating a real, IBM Watson-based, **social media** (**SM**) project:

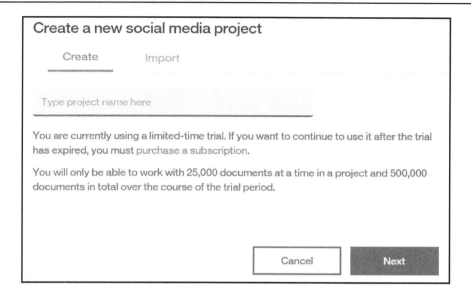

Once you have typed a name for your (SM) project, you can click **Next** to go to the page shown in the following screenshot, where you can define the details for your project:

Defining the details for your project

Refine

It's always all about the data, right? That is because having a thorough understanding of your data can actually make or break the outcome of a project.

Perhaps of all the out of the box features that IBM Watson delivers, the most important may just be **Refine**. Refine means just that—to hone, enhance, polish, improve or even perfect—the data you are planning to use in your IBM Watson project.

But why would you modify your data? Well, there are various reasons you may want to consider (or possibly need to) modify the data you are using. For example:

- You might want to enrich the data by adding calculations. Let's consider patient data that includes the physical characteristics of each patient, such has sex, height, weight, age, and so on. If you are interested in how various physical characterizes effect life expectancies, you may want to add a calculation that determines the patient's individual **body mass index** (**BMI**), which is calculated using height and weight. This ensures a consistent way of calculating BMI and also saves time by eliminating the need to perform the calculation within each analysis or prediction.
- Very often you may want to focus on a particular subset of your data. This can be accomplished by setting up a data filter (for that particular area of your business).
- More commonly, an exercise to make your data more readable is to rename columns or change a data type.
- Based upon your requirements or interest in the data, you may want to modify the default aggregations.
- Finally, you might want to create **hierarchies** and **groups** within your data.

Saving the original

As a rule, a proven practice when making any sort of change to your data file is to preserve the original state of the data. Not to worry, IBM Watson saves you the time and effort of backing up, saving, and then maintaining version control, since whenever you use **Refine**, a new and separate dataset is created automatically for you that is related to your original dataset.

Note: The changes that you make using **Refine** are saved as a separate version of the original dataset and are automatically available in **Predict**, **Explore**, and **Assemble**. If you modify the data in an exploration, the changed data is available only in that exploration.

In addition to using Refine to make your data more usable, you can also use Refine to learn more about your data. Once you are on the Refine page, you can click on the data metrics icon (it is the little bar graph on the left of the page), shown as follows:

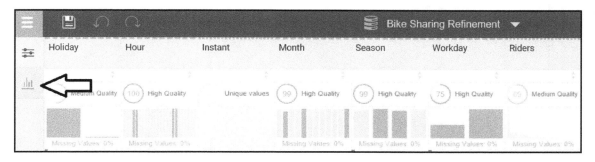

Bike sharing refinement

When you view the data metrics for your selected dataset, you will see the following information for each column of your data:

- The quality score for each column, which indicates a column's potential readiness for use in a prediction
- The percentage of data that is missing
- Distribution graphs of the data (in numeric columns)

Getting started with **Refine** is easy; once you click on **Refine**, a familiarly-formatted **Refine data set** dialog is presented (shown in the following screenshot), where you can select an existing dataset, add a new dataset, or take advantage of Watson's sample data:

After selecting (or uploading) a dataset, the data is displayed in the **Refine** page (shown in the following screenshot), where you can explore your data's metrics and perform the appropriate refinements based upon your requirements:

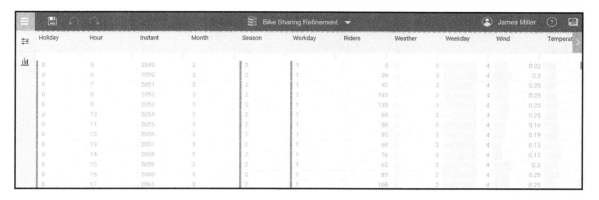

	Holiday	Hour	Instant	Month	Season	Workday	Riders	Weather	Weekday	Wind	Temperat
	0	5	2049	3	2	1	8	3	4	0.22	
	0	6	2050	3	2	1	36	3	4	0.3	
	0	7	2051	3	2	1	92	3	4	0.25	
	0	8	2052	3	2	1	192	2	4	0.25	
	0	9	2053	3	2	1	132	3	4	0.25	
	0	10	2054	3	2	1	69	3	4	0.25	
	0	11	2055	3	2	1	58	3	4	0.19	
	0	12	2056	3	2	1	90	3	4	0.19	
	0	13	2057	3	2	1	68	3	4	0.13	
	0	14	2058	3	2	1	76	3	4	0.13	
	0	15	2059	3	2	1	65	3	4	0.3	
	0	16	2060	3	2	1	85	2	4	0.25	
	0	17	2061	3	2	1	168	2	4	0.25	

Now that we've done the high-level, quick review of most of the fundamental features of the IBM Watson interface, and before we jump into our first IBM Watson project, let's move on to the final section of this chapter, where we will walk through the steps required to add some new data to IBM Watson as well as do some exploring and refining of that data.

Add – some data

You can add new data to IBM Watson easily. There is no need for extensive **Extract Transform Load** (ETL) scripting. The data can be contained in a cloud-based or on-premises database or simply uploaded to IBM Watson as a simple text file.

 You can also blend data you may have from multiple sources, view the quality of your data, and shape your data before you import it into IBM Watson Analytics.

The following steps can be followed to add data to Watson.

It goes without saying that the initial step is determine the source of the data that you want to use. We'll focus a lot more on this task in later chapters of this book, but for now, let's assume we have isolated a text file containing data we want to use in an IBM Watson project. So the steps are:

1. From the IBM Watson main page, click on **Add**, where you will have the option to **Create something new** or **add your data**:

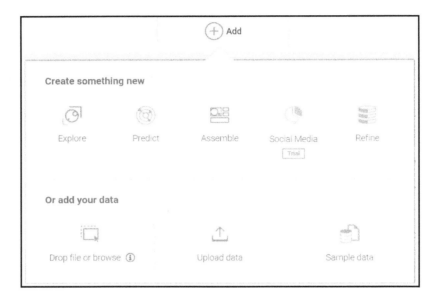

2. Once again, a similarly formatted decision dialog allows you to **Create something new** and **Or add your data**.
3. In this example, we'll click on **Upload data**. Watson will then display the following **Where is the data you want to upload?** dialog, where you can click on **Browse** (you'll notice that **Twitter** is also offered as a data source, but for now we can ignore that option):

4. After selecting **Browse**, you can navigate using a common file search dialog to the location of the data file that you want to upload to Watson. In the following screenshot, we have found our file named `Services Standards Results.csv` and clicked on it to select it:

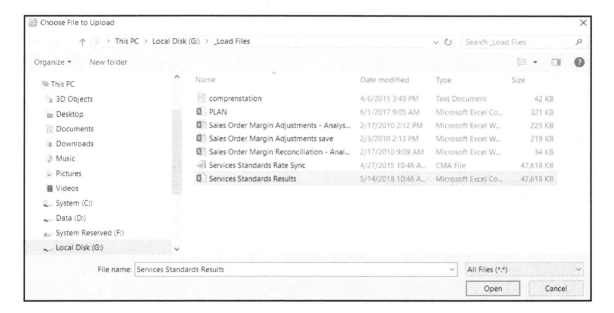

5. Once you select your file and click the button labeled **Open**, Watson will create an informational tile for your data file and begin **transferring...** the data:

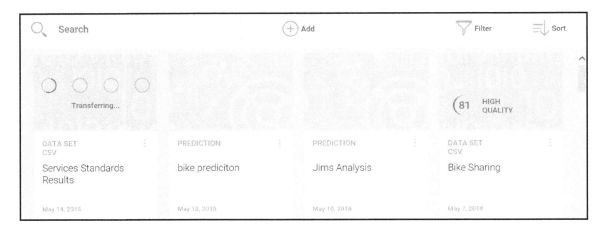

So, as you see, even without a programming or scripting expert's help, you can add data to your IBM Watson space, since Watson practically does that work for you!

Refine

One of the more important IBM Watson tasks is **Refine** (which we mentioned earlier in this chapter). Here will walk through the basics, using some Watson sample data:

1. From the **Quick-start** bar, click on **Refine**. From the **Refine data set** dialog, you then can scroll down and select **Sample data**; at this point you will see the **Sample data** dialog, which is displayed as follows:

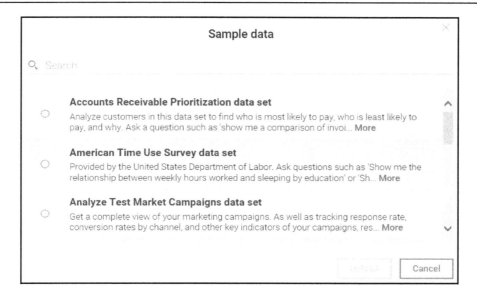

2. IBM Watson provides a nice list of sample data, each worth spending a bit of your time exploring and experimenting with. For now, let's pick **Bike Sharing data set** and then click on **Upload**:

To access the sample data it needs to be uploaded. Once uploaded it will appear as an informational tile (shown as follows) that can be selected and used:

3. Now that we have our data loaded and available, you can select it from the **Refine data set list**, which automatically loads it into the **Refine** page (which looks a lot like an Excel worksheet):

There are many tasks you can perform using **Refine**, such as:

- **General housekeeping**: Such as renaming columns, changing data types, or creating a subset of the data by filtering out irrelevant records
- **Summarization**: By altering the default aggregations
- **Enrichment**: By adding calculated fields, hierarchies and groups
- Review the metrics of the data, such as a quality score by data field or column

For now, let's assume we've made some of the previously-mentioned refinements to our data and want to save it as a new file. To do that, you simply click on the **SAVE** icon (looks such as a tiny diskette in the upper left of the page), enter an appropriate name for the new file, and click **Save** (on the **Save as** popup shown as follows):

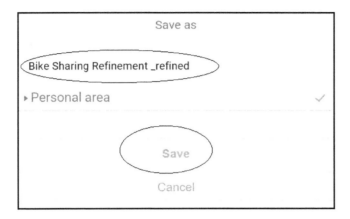

 If you are working in a multi-user environment, your new (refined) dataset is saved by default in your `personal` folder. To share your refined dataset with others, move it to a shared folder.

Summary

In this chapter, we started by defining the latest version of the IBM Watson Analytics platform and discussed the various objectives of the tool. In preparation for the projects reviewed in the upcoming chapters, we explored the Watson interface as well as the IBM Cloud console.

Finally, we reviewed some fundamental startup tasks (such as adding a new dataset, accessing Watson sample data, and refining an existing dataset) to ensure we are ready to proceed with our first Watson project!

In the next chapter, we will start with our first IBM Watson project use case.

A Basic Watson Project

2

In this chapter, we have elected to use a use case project that will analyze trip log data from a driving service company to determine which trip characteristics may have a direct effect on a trip's profitability, considering what type of trip is most profitable and which are prone to complications. This first Watson project serves to cover the basics of a simple Watson project—preparing the reader for upcoming, more complex projects presented in the following chapters.

We'll break down this first chapter into:

- The problem defined
- Getting started
- Building your Watson project
- Reviewing the results

The problem defined

As we said, we'll keep this first project example quite simple by focusing more on concepts and fundamentals, rather than spending time defining and exploring every detail (that will come in subsequent chapters!).

Let's start with some background. Suppose there is a group providing state-wide transportation services. This group originally began with a single driver, a car, and a van. Over time, the owner sold out to a group of investors who have evolved the company, now employing a large team of professional drivers and offering a full range of (driving) services for individuals and specific events, with vehicles chosen from an inventory of specialized vehicles. The owners are enjoying a steady business but not, unfortunately, steady profits. What can be done?

From the beginning, drivers had to log all information about each trip and submit that information to the main office to be paid and reimbursed for expenses. The information required by the drivers included dates, locations, events (types), customers (types), the kind of vehicle used, customer feedback, payment information, notes on any issues encountered, and so on. Since all of this information was required to be submitted before drivers received any payment, the information is believed to be complete and pretty reliable.

The investors are considering restructuring the business in an attempt to be more profitable, but a casual review of the trip reports doesn't seem to make sense.

For example, it would seem that the larger engagements—those that the company charges more for—should always be more profitable; however that doesn't seem to always be the case. In addition, some trips seem to be fraught with issues and some never are, customer satisfaction isn't predictable, some vehicles seem to always be requested while others seldom are, and the expected vehicle choices—based upon event type, locations, and so on—aren't always the ones used.

Even though having results (the number of trips, total sales, total costs, and so on) broken down in a variety of ways (event type, vehicle type, location, and so on)—is helpful, it falls short in answering questions such as:

1. When there are unplanned events (such as weather delays, mechanical failures, re-routing, and so on) that occur during a trip, they can still be profitable, but usually affect the original expected outcome. On what types of trip or under what types of scenario might these problems be expected to occur? As an example, do they happen more on trips that span 24 hours (overnight)?
2. Customer satisfaction and tip levels—what can be expected in terms of a gratuity offered as a tip, based upon the event or run? Do corporate events or trips with multiple destinations result in better tips (implying higher satisfaction)?
3. Could there be any correlation between the type of event and type of vehicle used? Do certain events demand a certain type of vehicle? Does the vehicle type influence the profitability of the trip?

These kinds of investigation are more cognitive in nature rather than the result of an aggregation, summary, or calculation. That being said, IBM Watson Analytics can be quite helpful.

Getting started

Recently, Stephen Archut, who has held the position of Product Marketing Manager, IBM Watson Analytics, indicated that the key capabilities of Watson Analytics include:

- Automated data discovery
- Exploration
- Guided predictive analytics
- Recommended visualizations
- Dashboard creation
- Visual storytelling

Further, he has said that these are all activities that business users perform on a daily basis and that Watson Analytics can accelerate. He also explained that Watson solutions aim to enhance, scale, and accelerate human expertise, targeting a wide range of complex challenges in the world today. Watson Analytics itself will understand, perceive, and relate information at a human level for your business problems, combining analytical insights with your expertise and experience to improve everyday decisions.

With these remarks in mind, we can get started with our project. Typically, one starts with understanding the need or objective (for doing the project). This was stated in the previous section. After that, a review of the fields available in your data is in order:

- **Run date**: The date the trip began/started
- **Pickup/Drop locations**: Where the customer was picked up and dropped off (drop-off could be different from the pickup location)
- **Primary and secondary destinations**: What the planned destinations were
- **Vehicle type**: The type of vehicle used for the trip
- **Event type**: For example, was this an athletic event, a wedding, a corporate event, and so on
- **Whether or not the trip was an overnighter**: If the driver and vehicle returned on the same day
- **A tip grade**: Not an amount, simply an indication of whether the customer tipped the driver an amount that was consistent with the cost and effort of the service and vehicle involved
- **Customer type**: Whether they were a new customer, referral, or existing
- **Guide**: If a tour guide was included in the trip

- **Issues**: Did any unplanned events occur on the trip—such as an accident or illness?
- **Type of payment**: Was payment paid through an invoice, check, or credit card

Gathering data

Once we've defined the problem and determined that we think that the available data contains values that are of interest, we can continue by building a project data pool (or a single, secure location for all the data we intend to use) to be input to our Watson project. This simply means that we consolidate or stitch together the organization's trip records into a single source, which can be a database table, OLAP cube, or a simple CSV text file.

The method used to create our data pool could be the topic of a chapter itself but again, for our first project, we'll keep it very simple and assume that we have a text file of all of our trip data and we are ready to proceed.

Building your Watson project

In this section we will go through a first project covering the basics of a simple Watson Analytics project, preparing you for upcoming, more complex projects presented in later chapters.

Loading your data

To actually start using Watson Analytics, go through the following steps:

1. You'll need to log in and, from the main or **Welcome** page, click on the **+Add** icon as shown in the following screenshot:

2. From there, you will see **Create something new** and **add your data**. Of course, we want to add our trip data, so we can choose between two methods: **Drop file** or **browse** or **Upload data**. Typically, for more realistically sized data files, you'll want to select Upload data and then browse to the file, rather than trying to **drag and drop** it:

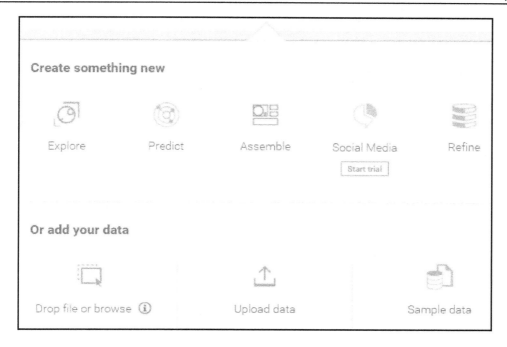

3. If you click on **Upload data**, Watson asks you **Where is the data you want to upload?**:

4. From there, you simply **Browse** to the location of your file and select it (using the normal Windows **Open** dialog):

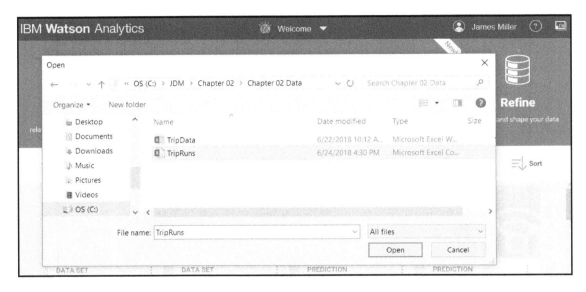

5. While uploading the file, IBM Watson Analytics analyzes the data as well as the metadata, creates hierarchies (from the metadata), and identifies concepts for use in your review. The data then appears on the **Welcome** page as a panel ready for you to get going!:

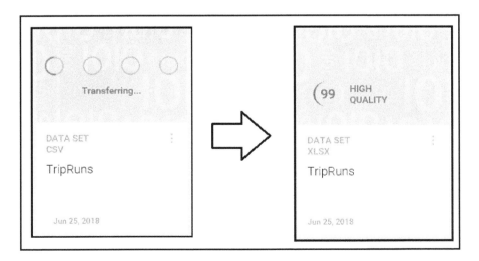

Depending upon the version of Watson you are using, you may also have the ability to connect to a data source directly.

6. If it does, once you select **Upload data**, you will have the opportunity to select a predefined data connection as your data source:

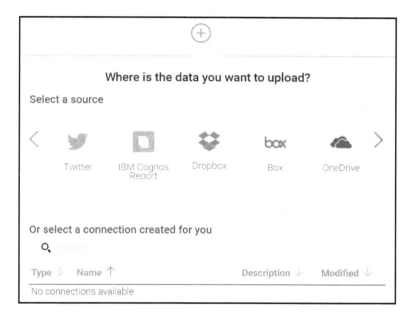

Data review

When you have successfully loaded your data into Watson Analytics, you should review it and assess its quality.

The IBM Watson Analytics documentation describes data quality as:

Data quality assesses the degree to which a data set is suitable for analysis. A shorthand representation of this assessment is the data quality score. The score is measured on a scale of 0-100, with 100 representing the highest possible data quality.

Further:

The data quality score for a data set is computed by averaging the data quality score for every column in the data set. Several factors affect the data quality score for an individual field or column.

The **factors** that can affect the data quality score include:

- **Missing values**: Records for which no data are entered.
- **Constant values**: Some fields have the same value recorded for every field.
- **Imbalance**: Occurs in a categorical field when records are not equally distributed across categories.
- **Influential categories**: Those categories that are significantly different from other categories.
- **Outliers**: Extreme values.
- **Skewness**: Skewness measures how symmetrical a continuous field is distributed. Skewed fields have lower data quality scores.

What does this mean?

The higher the data quality score is, the better the predictions that IBM Watson Analytics can provide.

If the quality of your data is low, the accuracy of the analyses in your explorations and predictions is less reliable.

Fortunately, you can improve the quality of your data with IBM Watson Analytics.

When data is loaded, Watson Analytics will read and analyze the data and determine a data quality score that describes the data's ability for making predictions. The higher the score, the better the data quality. If you provide a high-quality dataset, Watson Analytics provides a high data quality score.

You are able to see the score that is associated with each dataset in the list of assets on the Welcome page. As an example, a score of 68 indicates a dataset of medium quality. The lower the score, the higher the number of outliers or missing values and other issues.

To obtain a higher (data quality) score, clean your data (before you load it into Watson Analytics) by doing the following:

- Remove summary rows and columns from your data file
- Eliminate nested column headings and nested row headings

Load your data into Watson Analytics. Review the data quality score that is given to your dataset. If your data quality score is not satisfactory, repeat the cleaning process.

For more information, see *Optimizing the quality and usage of your data* within the online product documentation (https://watson.analytics.ibmcloud.com).

Improving your score with Refine

You can use the Watson Analytics **Refine** feature to work with data to both review and/or tweak it to improve its format and level of quality (take note that any changes that you might make are saved as a separate version of the original data).

1. To use Watson's **Refine** feature, you click on the **Refine** icon:

2. Watson will then open the **Refine data set** dialog, which it lists all of the available datasets. You can search for, or scroll-through, the list (of files) and then select the data to be refined by clicking on it:

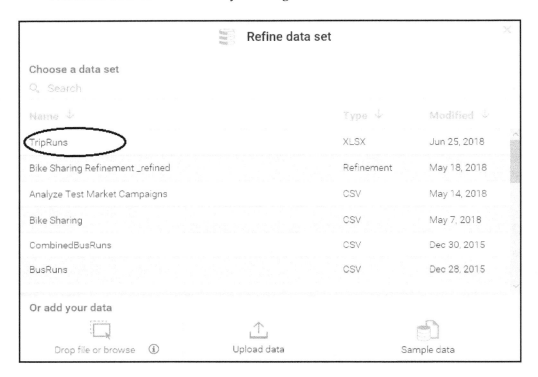

3. After selecting your data, the **Refinement** page is opened, showing your data:

Refining your data is sometimes referred to as tuning your data. In an earlier section of this chapter we talked about gathering your data using an external tool. During that process, transformations and reformatting can be done but typically; the work performed on the data at that time is rudimentary in nature, such as combining or merging files, aggregating, and summarizing. Conversely, once the data is loaded into Watson, the things you'll do will be more advanced.

For example, you might want to enrich the data by adding calculations (calculated fields), **filter** the data to a particular area of focus, or simply make data more usable by renaming columns, changing data types, and modifying the default aggregations. Finally, you might want to create hierarchies and groups within your dataset.

When you refine data in Watson Analytics, a new data file is created that is related to your original dataset, but always saved as a separate version of the original dataset.

One of the best uses for Watson Refine is to easily assess the quality of each column within your dataset. This is done by viewing the data metrics that Watson automatically provides. To access these Watson-provided metrics, you simply click on the **Data Metrics** icon:

Click on the Data metrics icon

The data metrics are displayed at the top of each column of data:

Quality of each column is indicated

As seen in the preceding screenshot, the metrics provided by Watson include a quality score for each column, which indicates a column's potential readiness for use in a Watson prediction (displayed as a numeric value in a green circle); the **percentage of data that is missing** from each column (written as text: missing values: 00%); and a **distribution graph** of the data in each numeric column (displayed as a black and white bar graph).

For now, let's look at a simple refinement. Suppose I would like to categorize my trip data into two groups: Day Trips and Overnights. We can do that easily using Watson Refine. To group the data, we can create a **Data group** column on the column named **Overnight**:

1. Click on the **Action** Icon:

2. Next, under the horizontal fields list (on the left of the page) click on the **Data group** icon:

3. Watson will display the **Data group** dialog (shown in the following screenshot). Here, you can click on the column name to select the column you want to create the group on (**Overnight**). Watson then will display the unique values found in that column. In this example, there are only two unique values: **Yes** and **No**:

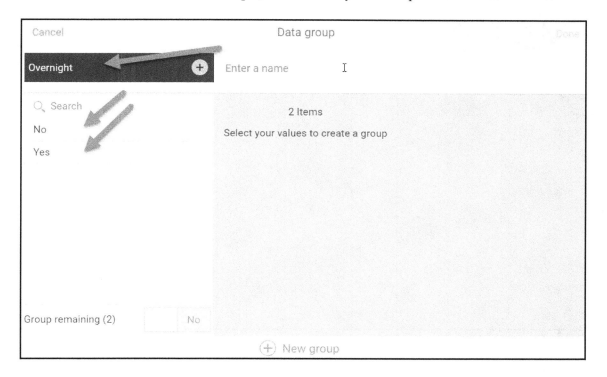

4. Next, click (to select) the value **No**, click on **New group**, type a name for this group, such as **DayTrip**, then click **OK**:

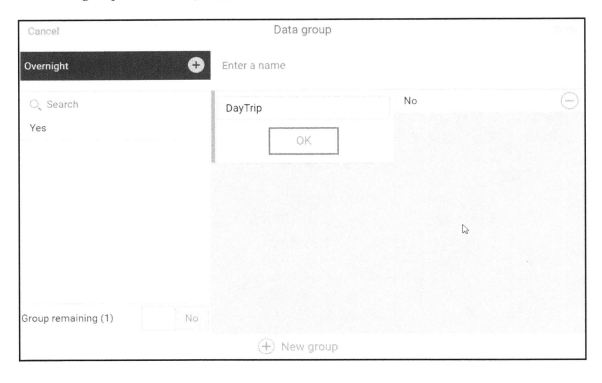

5. Notice that, in the preceding screenshot, on the lower left, Watson asks you, **Group remaining (1)**? Of course, we want to group the value, so click on **Yes.** Then once again click on **New group**, type the name of this group (**OverNighter**) and then click **OK**:

6. Finally, we need to **Enter a name** for our new column (you cannot leave this screen without one) so we enter `TripType` and then click **Done**:

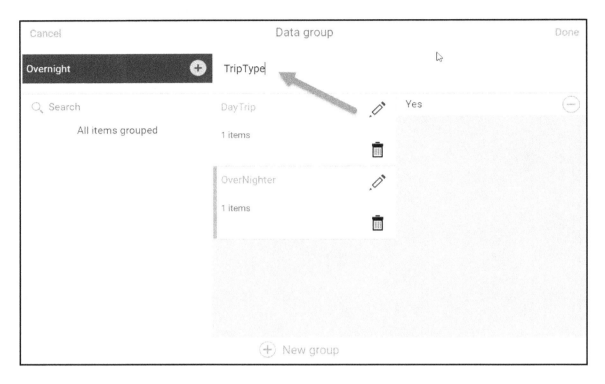

7. Now, our data group column **TripType** is part of our data set:

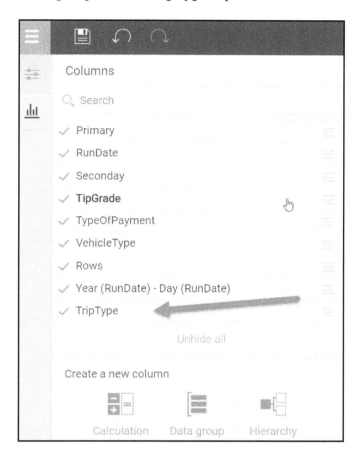

The objective of organizing your data into groups is to make the data easier to read and analyze. There are two kinds of group you can create in Watson, depending on the data type of the column (numeric or alphanumeric). We have just created an alphanumeric data group using the Yes/No raw data values. The group serves to make the data more readable, as **DayTrip** and **OverNighter** are perhaps more obvious than **No** and **Yes**. Another useful example of using a data group is on a numeric data column. With numeric columns, we can create groups that are ranges.

To illustrate, let's suppose that our organization's management purchased the firm in **2003**, so they want to group the trip data in two groups; one will be trips prior to the purchase (the years **2001** and **2002**) and the other group will be trips that occurred in **2003** and beyond:

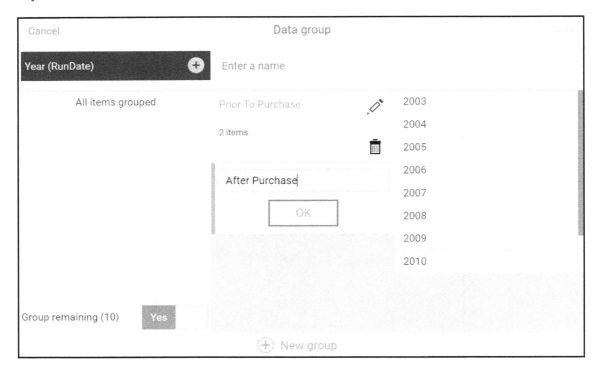

Refine or Explore

We should take note here that we jumped right into refining our data. Sometimes, especially if you are dealing with data completely new to you, you may spend time first exploring your data using the Watson Analytics Explore feature. We will spend time creating explorations later in this book, but for now it is good to mention, that if you refine a dataset, the changes that you make to it are available throughout Watson in Predict, Explore, and Assemble, but if you modify the data in an exploration, the changed data is available only in that exploration.

Creating a prediction

The objective of Watson Analytics is to give you the ability to create highly interpretable insights from your data based on complex modeling—without having to possess a deep understanding of each and every modeling algorithm.

Using Watson Predict, Watson Analytics uses these sophisticated algorithms to quickly and efficiently deliver predictions based on your data.

The predictions include visualizations and text descriptions of the analyses that Watson Analytics runs. You can use the visualizations to see analyses at a glance and read the text for supporting explanations and statistical details.

Because Watson Analytics automatically picks the right statistical tests for the data, you don't have to be know which test is best or which one to run.

1. To begin, go to the Watson Analytics **Welcome** page, and click on **Predict**:

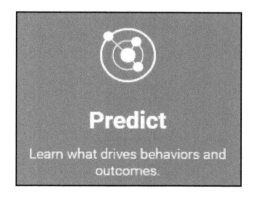

2. Watson will then display the **Create a prediction** dialog where you can select our (now refined) dataset, **TripRuns Refinement**, or the original, raw (before we refined or tuned the data set) **TripRuns**:

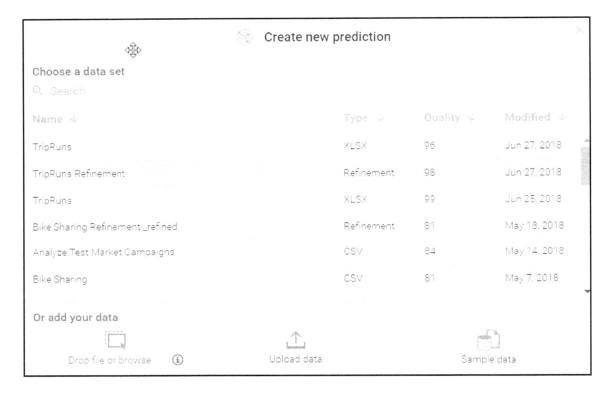

3. Once you select the data, you will be positioned at the **Create a new analysis** page:

Here, you'll start by typing a name for this prediction and then defining what you are interested in examining. To help understand how to define a prediction, let's supply a little background on Watson Analytics predictions:

- A Watson Analytics prediction is a container for a predictive analysis.
- A Watson Analytics prediction specifies the dataset that you are interested in.
- Each Watson Analytics prediction can have different targets and inputs.
- After you create a Watson Analytics prediction, you can view it to see the output from the analysis. The output consists of both visual and text insights.

So, let's now move on and create our Watson Analytics prediction!

We first must complete the **Name your workbook** field. Since our drivers are interested in being awarded tips from customers and we believe that the bigger the tip, the more satisfied a customer is (that is, disgruntled customers typically don't tip well!), let's call our prediction workbook `Tips Analysis`.

The next step is to **select target** (you can select up to five target fields that you want to predict). A target is a variable from your dataset that you want to understand. We are interested in **TipGrade** so we will select that from the **Select target** drop-down list where all of the column or field names in your data set should be listed:

The idea is that the target fields' outcomes may be influenced by other fields or columns within the data set. In other words, is there anything in the trip logs that can be used to predict how (or if) a customer will tip?

Once you click **Create**, Watson Analytics automatically analyzes the data as the last step in the creation of your prediction:

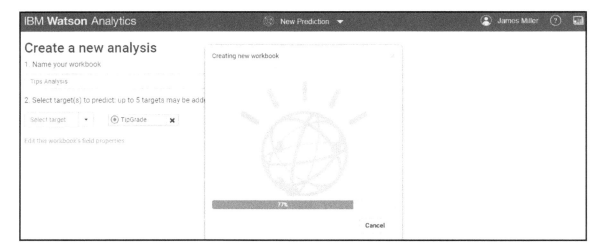

Top predictors

When the prediction is ready, you can view the results, starting with the **Top Predictors** page, where you can select a predictor that is interesting and open its visualization (in our example, the predictor is **Guide**):

Take a note that, on the **Top Predictors** page, the spiral visualization you see shows you the top predictors, in color. If there are multiple predictors, they appear in gray. The closer a predictor is to the center of the spiral, the stronger that predictor is. There is a visualization provided for each predictor found, giving you information about what drives each behavior and outcome. If you click on one of the predictors (or hover over it), you will see some details about it (as seen in the preceding screenshot).

Main Insight page

On the **Main Insight** page for the predictor that you chose (in our example there was just the one: **Guide**), you can examine the top insights that were derived from Watson's analysis:

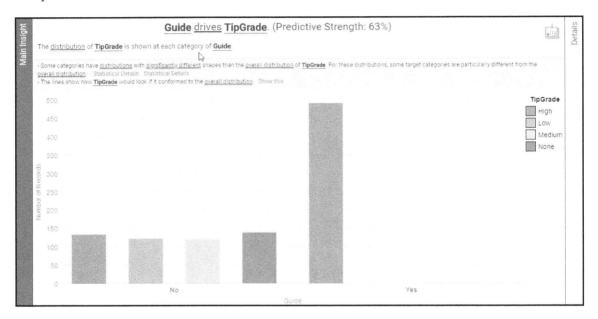

Details page

On the **Details** page you can drill into the details for the individual fields (**Guide** and **TripGrade**) and interactions:

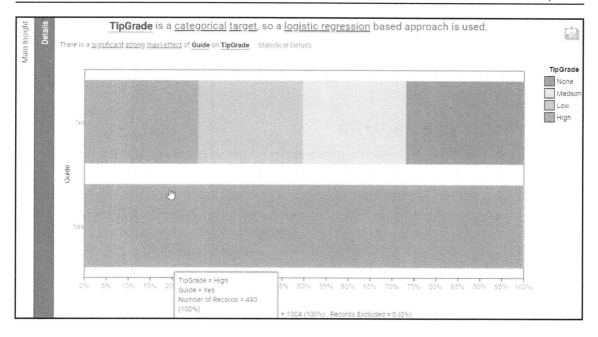

At the top of the details page, you should notice that Watson indicates the algorithm it used to find the insight and why:

TipGrade is a categorical target, so a logistic regression based approach is used.

If you click on the preceding terms (categorical, target, or logistic regression), Watson defines the term (and gives you a link to more details on the topic):

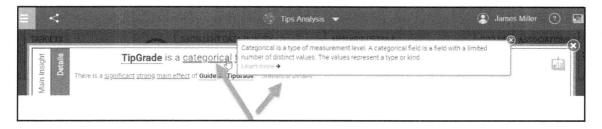

An insight

It would seem, given the results of our Watson Analytics prediction, that when a trip includes a trip guide, the tips are better (and perhaps the customer is more satisfied).

Reviewing the results

When you review a Watson Analytics prediction, you first see a summary of the most important insights Watson found within your data set. You also have the ability to easily explore specific fields in detail.

When you create your prediction, IBM Watson Analytics runs some analyses based on the data in your data set. The analyses focus on the targets that you set when you created the prediction.

There is a visualization for each key predictor, giving you information about what drives each behavior and outcome. If you tap one of the predictors (or hover over it), you see some details about it.

For example, the spiral visualization in our prediction visualization shows **Guide** just outside the center, which is the target for this prediction. The top predictor is represented in color. The strongest predictor (**Guide**) is indicated by the blue circle, and it is closest to the center of the spiral. The information box shows that **Guide** is the strongest predictor of **TipGrade**, with a **62.5% Predictive Strength**:

Each predictor that Watson Analytics found will have a corresponding snapshot visualization that contains information about the predictor and how it affects the target. The color of the circle in the spiral visualization is also found in the corresponding detailed visualization. In this example, the blue circle in the spiral visualization for the **Guide** predictor is included in the corresponding detailed visualization for **Guide**:

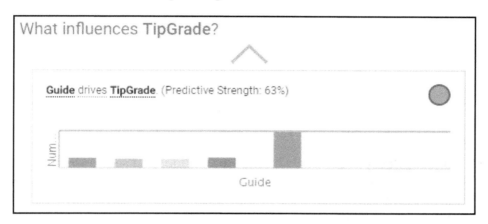

If you click on the visualization, you can see it in more detail on the **Main Insight** page:

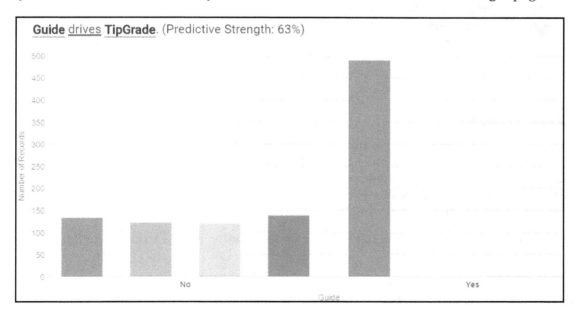

You can view more details about predictive insights that are hidden in the data. In the prediction scenario selector, you can specify how many fields you want to view that act as predictors for your target. For example, vehicle type and drop-off location, when combined, might be a predictor of **TipGrade**:

Selecting the fields

If you select **Two Fields**, you see a new set of visualizations and see how two variables might influence your target. If you select **Combination**, the visualizations provide a much deeper and more predictive analysis of your data by showing how a combination of variables influences your target.

 Note from the product documentation; as the prediction scenario selector indicates, choosing **One Field** leads to predictions that are perhaps easier to understand, but might be less predictive. Choosing **Combination** might lead to a prediction that is more accurate, but harder to understand. **Two Fields** might be somewhere in the middle.

Summary

In this chapter, we used a simple use case to cover the fundamental steps that are part of almost any Watson Analytics project. We started by stating an objective for the project by defining a realistic use case problem to solve, then gathered the data, loaded it into Watson Analytics (as an Excel Worksheet), and used Watson to refine the data before finally creating a prediction and reviewing the results.

At this point, the reader should have a clear understanding of how to create a Watson Analytics project.

In the next chapter, we will focus on analyzing how effective a supply chain is for a retail department store, using Watson Analytics in an attempt to isolate the causes of delivery performance.

An Automated Supply Chain Scenario

3

In this chapter, our use case project will focus on analyzing how effective a supply chain is for a retail department store. This automated supply chain scenario will look to provide insights into an organization's supply chain data and processes, in an attempt to isolate the cause of poor delivery performance.

We'll break down this chapter into these topics:

- The problem defined
- Getting started
- Building the project
- Reviewing the results

The problem defined

A supply chain is what it says: a chain or network of various resources who together share the objective of supplying a particular result or achieving a planned objective. These resources include (internal and external) organizations, people, activities, information, and raw materials involved in moving a product or service from a supplier to a customer.

Simply put, supply chain activities include transforming natural (and other) resources, raw materials, and components into a finished product that is then delivered to the end customer when the customer needs or wants it. So, it's not just minding inventory and shipping products. A supply chain is much more involved and complex.

Management of inventories goes beyond counting how many containers are sitting in a warehouse: it's a balancing act of keeping enough inventories on hand so that all customer and client expectations are met. Appropriate timing prevents delays; appropriate quantity prevents insufficient inventory while reducing the effect on profits.

Supply chain activities close to the raw material stage are known as **upstream activities** and activities between the manufacturer and end consumer are **downstream activities**. Typically, a supply chain is made up of multiple organizations that coordinate activities with the objective of setting themselves apart from the competition.

In today's business world, no stone can be left unturned in efforts to be solvent and better still, become and stay profitable. Smart firms recognize that effective supply chain management is an essential portion of their business model.

For this chapter's use case, let's pretend there is an organization named **Folly Surf** located in South Carolina in the US, which distributes surfboards. Their supply chain group is responsible for the procurement of the fundamental components of the product (the various types of surfboards) as well as assembly (which includes a process known as **shaping**), and finally delivery to the customer, who in this case is various independent surf shops who have placed orders for the boards.

In the years since its inception, born in some surfer's garage, the company's product has grown in popularity, driven by both the surfer's reputation and a high level of satisfaction (the board performs as advertised). This has increased demand beyond the company's ability to provide the product and is threatening not only short-term profitability but the company's future plans to expand its store locations.

Various efforts to improve operational efficiencies have had undesirable results.

For example, when deliveries are all on time, overall product quality has suffered, resulting in unhappy consumers and returns. When it is ensured that quality levels are met or exceeded, deliveries have been late, again resulting in unhappy customers and lost sales. Finally, when assembly teams are expanded, ensuring quality as well as the ability to deliver on time, the assembly team runs out of materials and parts.

Before things get too far out of control or beyond a repairable situation, the Folly Surf group is interested in seeing what insights can be identified with their data and Watson Analytics. So, using the Watson project methodology we identified in the previous chapter, let's jump in.

Getting started

Surfboard construction starts with a dense foam core and stringer, which is then covered with several layers of an epoxy resin, fiberglass, paint, and then finished with a high-gloss protective layer. Assembly also includes attaching one or more fins.

So, to define our supply chain, we have a list of materials:

- Foam core
- Stringer
- Resin
- Fiberglass
- Paint
- Protective treatment
- Fins and fin assembly

The materials listed here are shipped by a number of suppliers to one of two assembly facilities where the boards are fashioned and then sent to a warehouse where they are inventoried until ordered. Once an order is placed by the surf shop, the boards are picked, packed, and shipped and voila! – We have a supply chain that describes the chain management:

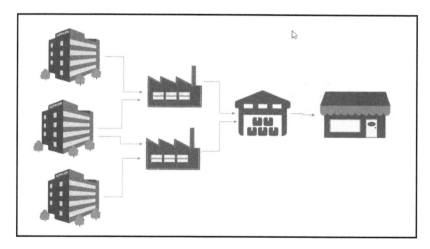

Supply chain describing the chain management

Although supply chain management has multiple objectives, we will focus in this chapter on one of the most fundamental: achieving efficient fulfillment. **Efficient fulfillment** is (perhaps loosely) described as making inventory readily available to the customer to fulfill demand. However, readily available must also be accompanied by the most efficient use of cross-chain resources, maintaining minimal inventory levels, ensuring little or no waste, and permitting the lowest costs overall.

In the next section, we will jump into the data from our imaginary surfboard scenario.

Gathering and reviewing data

Supply chain data is not singular in source, in that it is composed of a variety of informational data points and collections such as accounts payable, accounts receivable, manufacturing data, cost of goods sold, various vendor records, and so on.

This data is compiled using numerous methods and means, but in this book, we are focusing on analyzing data with Watson Analytics (not concocting or collecting the data), so we will assume that we have been provided with a file of supply chain data for analysis and proceed from there.

In the previous chapter's example project, we had a field-by-field description of the data we were going to use. In this chapter and this project, to start with we have only a provided file of supply chain data, and we have not been offered any further details as to what specifically is in the data file. What to do?

Although we could use an external tool to start examining the data, we know that Watson Analytics offers a really good exploration feature, so we will just go ahead and perform the steps to load our data.

Building the Watson project

Now, let's see how to build this project.

Loading your data

In `Chapter 2`, *A Basic Watson Project*, (in the *Loading Your Data* section), we loaded a file formatted as a Microsoft Excel worksheet. In this chapter, we will use those same steps to load our supply chain dataset. Rather than repeat those instructions here, we'll provide a few data-specific FAQs:

1. In practice, the most common file exchange format is either an Excel file or a **comma-separated** (**CSV**) text file, and Watson Analytics is happy with both formats, as long as you understand that Watson wants lists of data, not formatted report files (files containing nested rows or column headings, or total and subtotal rows).

2. In addition, there are different file size limits for each edition of Watson Analytics:

Edition	Maximum Rows	Maximum Columns
Free	100,000	50
Plus	1,000,000	256
Professional	10,000,000	500

File size limits for each edition

3. Additionally, when you upload (or add) a dataset in Excel worksheet form, Watson Analytics may ask you to provide additional details about your data file. For example, if a Microsoft Excel file contains several worksheets, you are prompted to select one worksheet to add; you might also be prompted to select a row to use as the column headings.

Note: You can refresh your memory of the steps required to add data to Watson Analytics by reviewing Chapter 2, *A Basic Watson Project* or visiting the following online reference: https://www.ibm.com/support/knowledgecenter/SS4QC9/com.ibm.solutions.wa_an_overview.2.0.0.doc/wa_an_hlp_data_new.html.

Reviewing the data

Datasets loaded into Watson Analytics are sometimes referred to as assets. Our supply chain asset (a CSV file named SuperSupplyChain.csv) is now loaded and ready for review:

Loading the data

As you can you see, already Watson Analytics has created the **SuperSupplyChain** panel and starts our review by giving us a data quality rating of (only) 67 percent. In Watson Analytics, we can perhaps start with an **Explore**.

An **Explore** creates powerful visualizations on your data to help you discover patterns and relationships that may impact your business, find new insights, or at least help you identify new questions that you can ask of your data.

To initiate an **Explore**, click on the **Explore** image in the upper left of the **Welcome** page (shown in the following screenshot):

Explore button on the Welcome page

After clicking **Explore**, we can locate and select our `SuperSupplyChain` file:

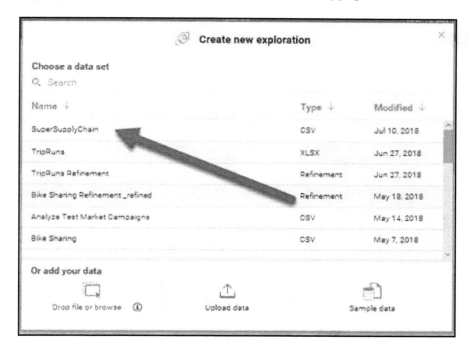

Selecting SuperSupplychain file

At this point, Watson Analytics explores your data and presents its findings as a page of entry points or prompts:

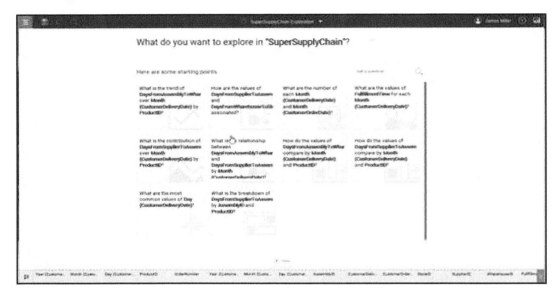

Watson Analytics exploring the SuperSupplychain options

For example, Watson prompts **What are the values of FullfillmentTime for each Month(CustomerDeliveryDate)?**:

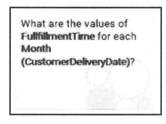

An example of what's reflected in the Watson Analytics option

To see the answer to that question (or the results of running a query to retrieve these values), you just click on the question and Watson runs the query for you and presents the results in an awesome visualization:

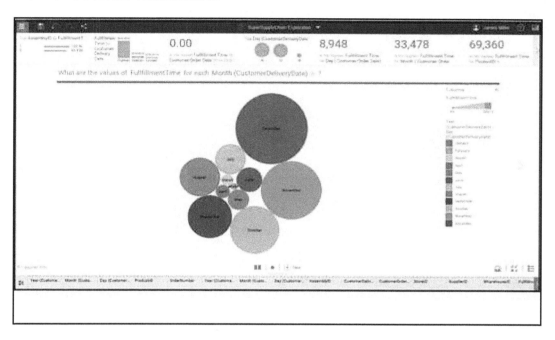

Watson Analytics displaying the query results

To me, it appears that it takes longer on average to fulfill an order placed in December or November, which may make sense if we consider those months are perhaps known for **holiday gifting**.

You can see the Watson Analytics added value clearly here. Watson automates the process of having to do the following:

1. Think of a question (query)
2. Formulate a query based upon the question
3. Execute the query
4. Review resultant data
5. Think of an appropriate visualization type
6. Create the visualization using the query's result
7. Draw a conclusion

Although it is helpful for Watson to provide this insight, the conclusion that holiday months have longer fulfillment times seems common sense. So, let's do some more exploring. I have a theory, based upon some rumors, that the bottleneck in fulfillment is the assembly plants. To confirm that using Watson, we can create a new page by clicking on **New**:

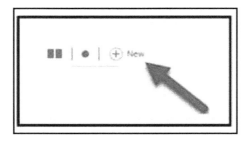

Creating a New page

You can enter a new question for Watson Analytics in several ways:

- On the **Welcome** page, click a dataset and enter a question
- On the **Welcome** page, click **Explore**, select a dataset, and enter a question
- On the **Welcome** page, click **Add**, tap **Exploration**, select a dataset, and enter a question
- In **Explore**, click **New** and enter a question

Next, back at the **prompt** page, we can enter our own question (or answer to the question: **What do you want to explore next?**) into the search bar:

```
does assemblyid impact fullfillmenttime?
```

Notice as we type Watson auto fills the column names from our file and quickly generates a new list of exploration prompts related to our question (Watson Analytics matches the words you type in your question to the column headings in your dataset):

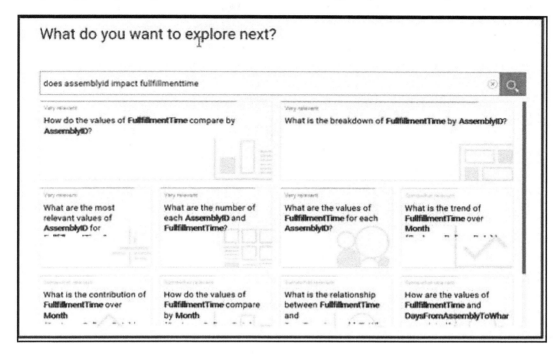

Watson Analytics exploring the options

Right away in the top left, I spy a **Very relevant** prompt: **How do the values of FullfillmentTime compare by AssemblyID**. Since **FullfillmentTime** is the performance statistic we want to improve on, and we have a notion that one or other assembly plants may be a problem, this prompt does seem relevant. Again, we can drill into the topic by clicking on it:

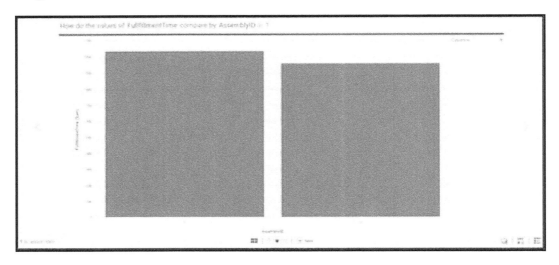

Watson Analytics reflecting the comparison result

From this visualization, it appears that the assembly plants both impact fulfillment times pretty equally (or at least I don't see a material difference between the two).

For the sake of brevity, I will tell you that exploring suppliers yielded a similar conclusion, as well as products. So, if the different suppliers, assemblers, or products do not uniquely impact fulfillment times, what does?

Well, it's not too much of a stretch to consider that instead of comparing the performance of the different suppliers or the performance of the different assemblers, perhaps we should see if there is any disparity between the time it takes for materials to arrive from suppliers (to the assembly plants) and the time it takes for the assembled product to arrive from the assemblers (to the warehouse):

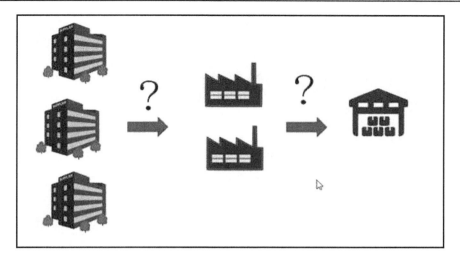

Time needed to supply materials

So, we might think of this question as follows: is there a material difference between the time it takes for a supplier to ship materials to an assembly plant and the time it takes for an assembly plant to ship assembled product to the warehouse? Thinking in Watson terms, since we have columns of data that contain these totals, we might type our query as follows:

```
how does daysfromsuppliertoassembly compare to
daysfromassemblytowarehouse
```

The following screenshot shows the entered question:

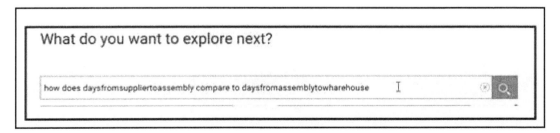

Question can be asked to explore Watson Analytics

From there, Watson Analytics gives us the following (**Very relevant**) prompt:

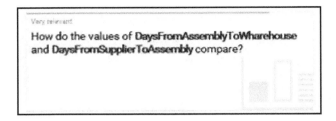

Prompt displaying the explore result

And if you drill into this prompt, Watson Analytics provides the following visualization:

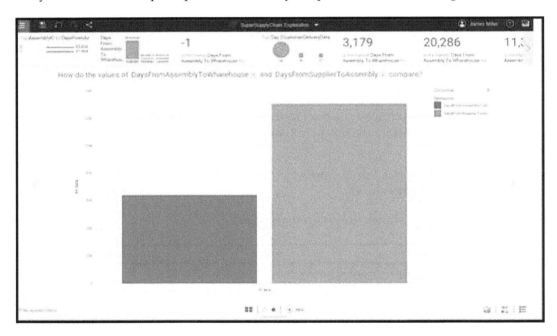

Visualization reflected by Watson Analytics

After reviewing this visualization, we might conclude that the time required to ship materials from any supplier to either assembly plant can be (perhaps materially) longer then on average the time that has been required to ship the assembled product to the warehouse. But is this the case? Do all suppliers perform equally? Perhaps Watson can answer this.

Suppose we start by posing the question `What is the value of DaysFromSupplierToAssembly?`. Watson Analytics produces the following (not very interesting) visualization:

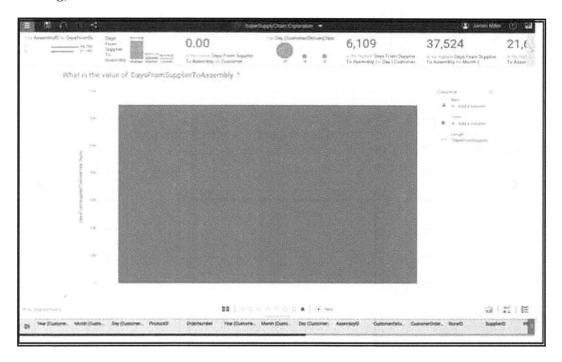

What is the value of DaysFromSupplierToAssembly? Visualization

Again, not a very interesting graphic, but if we click on + **Add a column** (under **Columns** | **Bars**, shown here), we can improve our visualization:

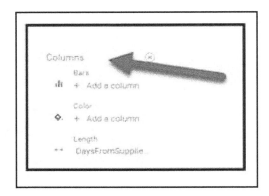

Add a column to improve visualization

At this point, Watson Analytics provides a list of the columns in our data file. We are concerned at this point with suppliers, and that column is not listed, so I can type the column name and search for it:

Searching for relevant columns

Once the column name **SupplierID** comes up, you can click on it to select it and have Watson Analytics add that column name to the visualization. Now, the graphic is much more interesting:

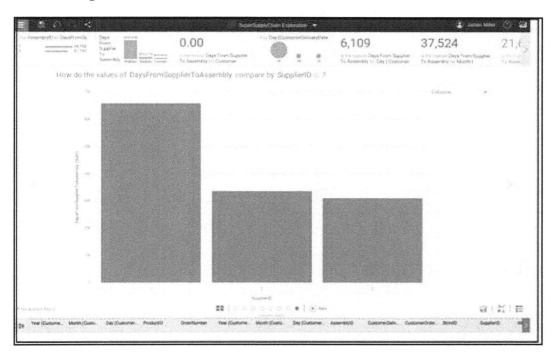

Adding SupplierID column name to visualization

From this visualization, we may understand that supplier number 1 is typically slower in fulfilling its orders than supplier 2 and supplier 3. So, now we have become aware that the number of days it takes to fulfill a customer's order (or the number of days the customer has to wait for the surfboard they ordered) is often affected by waiting for materials to be sent by suppliers to the assembly plants, not the time it takes to assemble the product, and there is a particular supplier that appears to have the most delays. Now, we have an actionable insight into improving supply chain performance.

As you can see, while you are performing data explorations, Watson Analytics helps you uncover not only answers in your data (which lead to making better decisions) but perhaps even more questions. Watson's ability to quickly provide powerful visualizations is the key to recognizing patterns within the data you are exploring. Watson allows you to refine each of the visualizations in different ways and as you do so, Watson Analytics updates the graphic to relate to the new context that you are examining.

Once you become comfortable that you have gained an important insight through a particular visualization, you'll probably want to share it later. You can set aside interesting or important visualizations created from Explore. You can then add the visualizations to the dashboards and stories that you create in Assemble (which we will cover in the Sharing section later in this chapter). Visualizations saved from Explore remain interactive when you add them to a dashboard or story. You can also change the data that's displayed in the visualization in Assemble in the same ways that you edit it in Explore.

To save a visualization, you simply click on the **Collection** icon (shown here) to add the visualization to the collection:

Selecting collection icon

Refining the data

In Chapter 2, *A Basic Watson Project* of this book, we took the time to use the Watson Analytics Refine feature to tune a dataset, as well as talk about some of the things you can use Refine for. Since we have identified an insight while exploring our data in this chapter, we won't revisit Refine here, but rest assured we will revisit Refine later in this book.

Creating a prediction

Obtaining analytical insights from data with Watson Analytics is accomplished with the Predict feature. The steps for creating a prediction are simple. These steps are referred to as a **Prediction Workflow**. This workflow is outlined in the Watson documentation and is worth reviewing here (at a higher level, perhaps):

1. Add data.
2. Click on **Prediction**.
3. Select (up to five) target fields that you want to predict. A target is a variable from your dataset that you want to understand. The target field's outcomes are influenced by other fields in the data.

Note: If you are not sure which field should be the target, you can let Watson Analytics automatically select the target.

4. Click **Create.** Watson Analytics then automatically analyzes the data as it creates the prediction.
5. When the analysis is completed, view the results. On the Top **Predictors** page, you can select a predictor that is interesting and open its visualization.
6. On the **Main Insight** page (for the predictor that you chose in step 5), you can examine the top insights that were derived from the analysis.
7. Go to the **Details** page to drill into the details for the individual fields and interactions.

Supply chain prediction

Now that we have explored our supply chain data and identified an insight that we think is worthwhile, let's go ahead and use the data to create a Watson Analytics prediction, like so:

1. From the **Welcome** page, click on **Predict**:

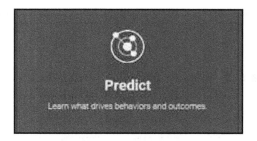

Predict icon

2. Choose our file:

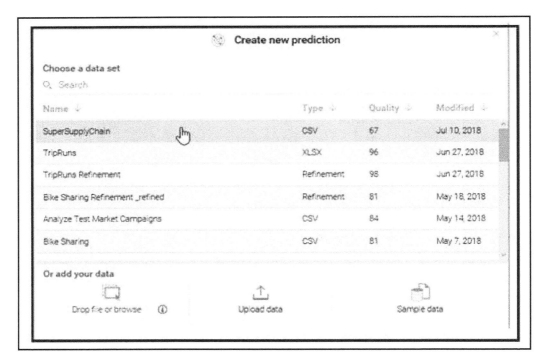

Selecting our file for prediction

3. On the **Create a new analysis page** (shown next), provide a name for our prediction, select the column named **FullfillmentTime** as our target, and then click **Create**:

Creating a new analysis- FullfillmentTime

Watson Analytics creates our prediction for us:

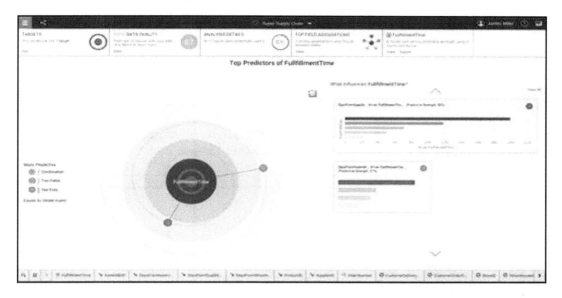

Watson Analytics creating our prediction

Predictors

It's important to first settle on a definition for a predictor. Generally, the following is accepted.

A predictor variable is a variable that can be used to predict the value of another variable (as in statistical regression)

`www.thefreedictionary.com/predictor+variable`

When you open a prediction, the **Top Predictors** page appears. The spiral visualization you see shows you the top key drivers or predictors (in color, with other predictors in gray). The closer the predictor is to the center of the spiral, the stronger that predictor is.

There is a visualization generated for each key predictor, giving you information about what drives each behavior and outcome. If you click on one of the predictors (or hover over it), you can see some details about it. Each predictor has a corresponding snapshot visualization that contains information about the predictor and how it affects the target. The color of the circle in the spiral visualization is also found in the corresponding detailed visualization.

In our prediction, the blue circle in the spiral visualization for the **DaysFromSupplierToAssembly** predictor is included in the corresponding detailed visualization for **DaysFromSupplierToAssembly** (shown here) and if you click on the visualization, you can see it in more detail on the **Main Insight** page:

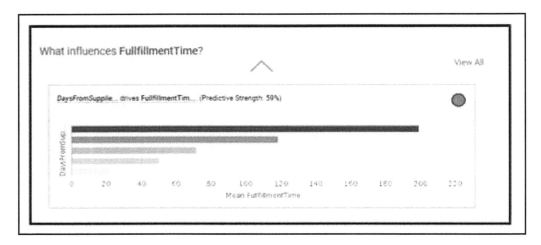

Visualization for DaysFromSupplierToAssembly

Once Watson has created a prediction, you are not locked in to what you specified on the **Create a New Analysis** page. You can dive deeper using the prediction scenario selector (shown here) to specify how many fields you want to view that act as predictors for your target. In our prediction, what might we combine with DaysFromSupplierToAssembly to be a more exact predictor of fulfillment time?

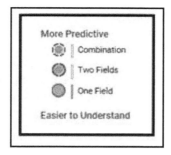

Selecting fields

If you select **Two Fields**, you see a new set of visualizations and see how those two variables influence the target. If you select **Combination**, the visualizations provide a deeper and more predictive analysis, displaying how a combination of the variables influences the target.

 Note: As the prediction scenario selector indicates, choosing **One Field** leads to predictions that are easier to understand, but might be less predictive. Choosing **Combination** might lead to a prediction that is more accurate, but harder to understand. **Two Fields** might be somewhere in the middle.

Main insights

The results of predictions in Watson Analytics are presented as a combination of both visual and text insights. Text insights describe the results of the Watson Analytics analysis. Visual insights are visualizations that support the text insights. All of the insights are prearranged into insight sets to make them easier to digest.

 Note: In addition to text and visual insights, dynamic visual insights are dynamic changes to the visualization that result from expanding a text insight.

In our supply chain prediction, we started with a presupposition that the cause of increasingly longer order delivery times was due to a problem at the assembly plants. After creating an exploration, we saw first that delivery times increased during November and December, but that was expected, due to higher order volumes. Next, we compared the performance of each assembly plant and found that they performed pretty much the same. From there, we checked for different performance levels of each supplier and also explored products, to see whether a specific product required additional lead time.

Finally, we found that there is a difference between the time it takes to ship materials from suppliers to the assembly plants and the time required to ship assembled product from the assembly plants to the warehouse.

With this awareness in mind, we then created a Watson Analytics prediction using the **FullfillmentTime** column as the target. In the following section, we will examine how to save and share the results in more detail.

Reviewing the results

Earlier in this chapter, we touched on Watson Analytics Collections. We showed how to save our visualization as an asset for later use. You can save assets similarly from Explore, Predict, and Assemble.

But what is Assemble? We haven't covered it yet. You use the Assemble capability in Watson Analytics to convey the analysis and insights discovered in Predict and Explore. You can use Assemble to assemble Watson assets, as well as external files (such as images), into Watson interactive views. Views can be either dashboards or stories and can be easily shared with others.

Dashboards display a particular view while stories deal with time or state; in other words, you would expect a story to depict a change over a period of time, or a before-and-after state of something. The best way to learn is to do, so in the next section, we will create a dashboard to show our supply chain insight!

Sharing with a dashboard

A Watson Analytics dashboard is a kind of view that helps you to monitor events or activities at a glance by providing key insights and analysis about data on one or more pages or screens. Types of dashboards include single page, tabbed, and infographic.

1. To create a Watson dashboard, from the **Welcome** page, click on **Assemble**:

Assemble icon

2. Next, you will see the **Create new view** page (shown next) where you can select the data file to build the dashboard from:

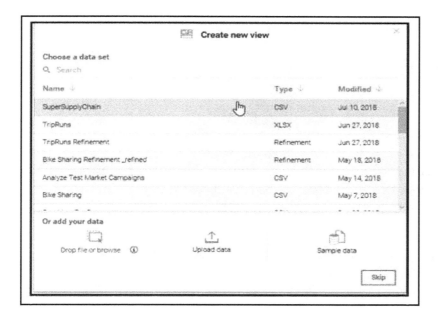

Selecting our data

Hint: If you didn't have a dataset in mind, you can just click on **Skip**.

3. The next page that you'll see is the **Create** page, which is shown here:

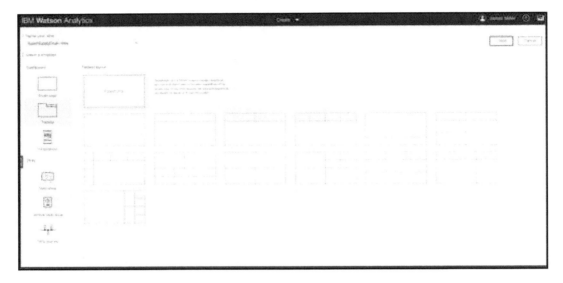

Create page

4. On this page, you have to do two things: provide a name for the view and select a template or style for your dashboard. For the name, if you select a data file, the name of the view defaults to the name of the dataset, but you can change that name just by typing the new name you want into the **Name your view** field.

5. Under **Dashboard** (down the left side of the page), you need to select a dashboard type. The types are **Single** page, **Tabbed,** or **Infographic** (these types are described in detail in the Watson online documentation).

6. Once you click on the dashboard type you want, click **Create**. You will then notice that across the bottom of the page the dataset icon, name of the dataset, and data columns are displayed:

The dataset icon, name of the dataset, and data columns are displayed

7. Across the top of the page, you will see this:

Options at top of the page

Now, you are ready to construct an Watson Analytics dashboard. The icons you see in the gray bar space (shown in the preceding screenshot) are pretty self explanatory: **Visualizations**, **Text**, **Media**, **Webpage**, **Image**, **Shapes,** and **Properties**; it is also easy to click on and try each of them.

I've selected a single page dashboard template and then the **Freeform** layout. Freeform allows me to place and size visualizations and other assets exactly where and how I want them to appear on my dashboard. The next step should be to verify my dashboard properties. Watson Analytics provides the ability to select a theme as well as a general style. These properties are accessed by clicking on the properties icon:

Watson Analytics displaying properties icon

I am happy with the default settings at this time, so we'll not change any dashboard properties. We can add a collected asset to our dashboard with just a drag and drop, but first let's build a new visualization from scratch.

Adding a new visualization

To build a new visualization, first click on the **Visualization** icon (shown here) and then click on the type of visualization you want:

Visualization options

Once you select your visualization type, Watson will add a visualization frame to the dashboard, ready for you to set the properties of the visualization:

set the properties of the visualization

In the visualization frame, you can set the **Axis label**, **Color by,** and **Value** columns by dragging column names from the data tray (as we mentioned earlier in this section, the data tray is across the bottom of the dashboard) to the visualization frame. In the following screenshot, I have used the columns **FullfillmentTime** and **Month**:

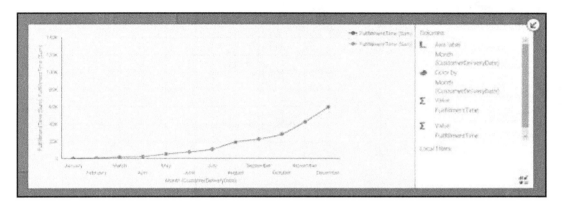

Adding columns

As you drop in your selected column names, Watson will dynamically build and display the visualization; this helps you decide whether you are using the correct columns from your data. When you are happy with the visualization, click the **down arrow** icon on the edge of the visualization to save it to the dashboard. You can, at any time, select the visualization and resize it, move it within the dashboard, or remove it from the dashboard.

In the following screenshot, you can see our dashboard with the saved visualization. In addition, I have used the **Text** icon to add a heading above our visualization. Finally, note that the data tray is visible across the bottom of the dashboard:

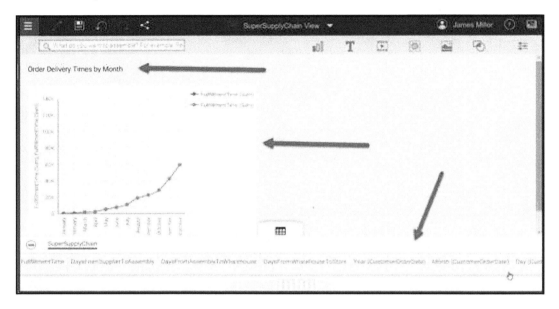

Dashboard with the saved visualization

Now that I have added a visualization, we can see that it has a white background, which is in contrast to the light gray background, so I will go back to the **Properties** icon and under **General style**, switch the dashboard background to white:

Now that we have seen how to create a new visualization in our dashboard, let's see how to add a collected asset. If you click on the **Collection** icon (in the upper right corner of the page), Watson displays your Asset Library, which you can scroll through and determine which asset you'd like to add to your dashboard:

Watson displaying your Asset Library

Watson displays the Asset Library as follows:

Selecting the required asset

You can click to select the asset you'd like to add to your dashboard and then drag and drop it onto the dashboard. You're done. Watson adds it; you can then resize it and place it as you wish.

Let's add a title for the asset we just added. This time rather, than using the **Text** icon, we will click on the label we had already added and click on the duplicate icon:

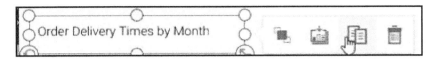

Clicking on duplicate icon

Watson will make a copy of the title, in which you can change the text and move it over the asset we added earlier.

The following screenshot is our finished dashboard:

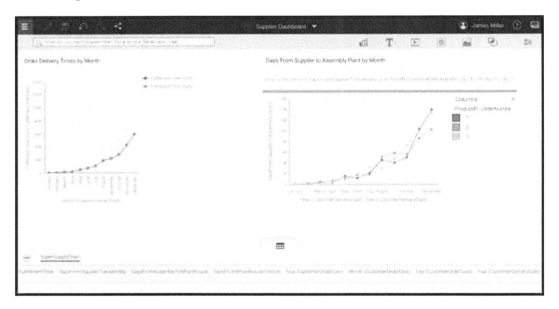

Final Dashboard view

Our dashboard looks pretty nice, so let's save it by clicking the **Save** icon in the upper left of the page, then typing a name for the dashboard in the **Save as** popup:

Saving the dashboard

Now that we have constructed and saved a nice Watson dashboard, we should share it. You can share your Watson Analytics insights with anyone, even those who do not have access to Watson. To do this, you can download the insights as a file.

 Note: For fellow Watson Analytics users, you can also share a direct URL link to an exploration, prediction, or view that can be accessed only by other Watson Analytics users in the same account.

Watson Analytics currently supports the following file formats:

- PNG image
- Microsoft PowerPoint presentation, PPT; you can share presentations only if you use the Plus edition or Professional edition of Watson Analytics
- Adobe PDF

The easiest way is to click on the **Share** icon and select from the supported formats. I want to be able to print copies of my dashboard to hand out at the next Surfboard store manager's meeting, so I will select PDF:

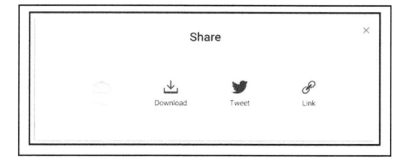

Selecting options to share/print the dashboard

Once you select the PDF format, you can provide a name for your PDF file, then click
Download:

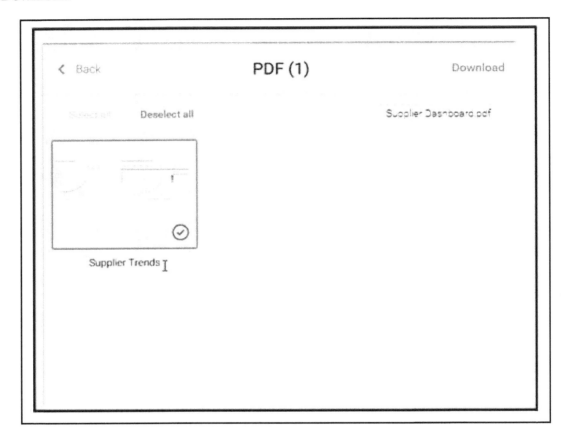

Downloading the PDF file

Summary

In this chapter, we introduced an imaginary custom surfboard company and its supply
chain process. Given the firm's objective of improving on the time it takes to fill customer
orders, the chapter went through a Watson Analytics project that focused on its supply
chain and a perceived problem with assembling the boards on time. After analysis, we saw
that the issue was really with suppliers, not assemblers, a key insight isolating the cause of
delivery performance.

Healthcare Dialoguing

4

In this chapter, we will look at Watson's cognitive assistance solution, specifically as regards creating an engaging dialog between healthcare providers and their patients. This project will involve establishing relevant recommendations based upon patient inputs.

This chapter will contain the following topics:

- The problem defined
- Getting started
- Building the project
- Reviewing the results

The problem defined

Once again, we'll start this chapter by defining the problem—or opportunity—before us. First, some background. Some of the most valuable data out there (when it comes to an individual's well-being) is healthcare data.

Typically, healthcare data or health information is defined as data relating to a person's medical history, which includes symptoms, diagnoses, procedures, and outcomes. The purpose of this healthcare information is to provide useful and meaningful insights so that it can be used properly and effectively to achieve an objective.

When we think about using data and software to improve healthcare as an objective, our first thought is usually about reducing the cost of healthcare, but another goal that has emerged recently has been to improve the overall health of individuals by perhaps identifying a person's health risks sooner, rather than focusing on a diagnosis that is based upon reported or observed symptoms. This idea proposes using resources for *health*care rather than sickcare:

> *During the history of medicine, we have not been involved in healthcare; no, we've been consumed by sickcare. We wait until someone is sick and then try to treat that person. Instead, we need to learn how to avoid illness and learn what will make us healthy.*
>
> Linda A. Winters-Miner, PhD.

Suppose that we add to the availability of this information (specifically medical histories) a different form of information known as **patient-dialoguing** data?

What is dialoguing?

Patient dialoguing can help the healthcare treatment process evolve from a caregiver listing a patient's symptoms and then applying appropriate treatments, to a healthcare professional identifying risks and making predictive recommendations.

Although you may have read that genomics (that is, the examination of DNA) is set to play a key role in the shift toward better health and the prevention of illness, we will consider the collection and analysis of patient dialog information as playing an integral part of this evolutionary shift.

u data consist of statements that are made between patients and healthcare providers, including naturally occurring narratives that are shared by patients with their physicians at key decision points along the patient's journey. Some of these narratives include what is known as an **illness narrative** from an exam-room interchange, in-home ethnography, and follow-up interviews and questionnaires. Make no mistake, there is value in the way that patients speak and feel about their illnesses and interact with your treatments.

Dialog data characteristics include the following:

- What are the symptoms that are reported by the patients?
- How long is the average physician–patient conversation?
- How is the conversational time split up between patients, physicians, and caregivers?
- What are the top questions asked by patients?
- What are the top questions asked by physicians?
- What are the conversation initiation frequencies?
- What are the dialog capture mechanisms used?
- How much of the dialog is format-based and how much is free form or free flowing?

Leveraging (new) data to identify risk

For some time now, the public has embraced the idea that patients who are engaged in their own care and well-being are ultimately healthier than those who are not active in that role. In fact, health insurance companies have worked to increase individuals' engagement levels by creating incentives, social media campaigns, and targeted education that aims to encourage healthier lifestyles, regular wellness visits, and chronic disease management, all with the objective of educating beneficiaries on the critical role they play in preserving their own health.

As these programs take hold, there is the opportunity for a dialoguing process, as well as using that dialog to glean new insights. The investigation and measurement of this type of information is an exciting prospect, and part of an evolution from delivering care *to* patients to partnering *with* patients to prevent unhealthy consequences.

In the next section, we will describe a dataset that is derived from various patient dialoguing sessions.

Getting started

In this section, we have made a hypothetical, yet hopefully realistic, setting where the reader can identify a goal, determine what data is available for use, and then review, understand, and load that data into Watson Analytics. We will be looking at a scenario where you have been given access to patient medical records, as well as the legends from various dialog sessions with those patients.

Although dialoguing isn't always saved in a formatted (or at least consistently formatted) way, it is easiest to consume and use dialoguing with Watson Analytics if some time is taken to apply at least some degree of formatting to the data. The amount of effort required to format or apply formatting to dialog information depends (mostly) on the method that was used to collect it.

Gathering and reviewing data

The data for this project consists of three types: system-based medical history, automated dialog content, and physician observations. This is illustrated in the following diagram:

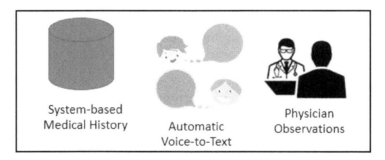

The system-based patient medical history columns within our data include common data points, such as sex, age, height and weight, medical conditions, past treatments, allergies, and so on (we will see more detail on this in a later section of this chapter, as we begin working with the data). The new information, the data that we are most interested in, is the content of the patient dialog and physician observations.

This information has been collected using a combination of voice-to-text technology, as well as information manually entered by the physician during the dialog session with the patient and perhaps after the dialog is completed.

The combination of these two nicely complementing datacapture methods provides us with a flexible structure to capture the information for later use without allowing the conversation to stray too far from the point, while also not forcing a rigid dialog, since it is imperative that the patient have the freedom of (almost) complete expression.

As we will see, the dialog content will include the patient's view of things, such as the symptoms that they feel they are experiencing, their level of discomfort, their description of their lifestyle—including their admission of whether or not they use alcohol or drugs—personal family health history, and even what they feel should be the prognoses and/or treatment.

As we've already mentioned earlier in this chapter, oftentimes, the ability to review and understand the data using IBM Watson Analytics requires various preprocessing activities. At some point, the ability to do all of that preprocessing in Watson Analytics may be possible, but at the time of writing, it's best to do this outside of Watson.

We'll start this Watson Analytics project with the assumption that minimal preprocessing has already taken place, and we are ready to load the data into Watson.

However, we will soon see that, although the data is somewhat preprocessed/preformatted for us, there will be additional refinement required once the data is loaded.

Building the project

First, we'll pull in or load our dialog data file. If we sneak a peek at a portion of the dialog section of the file, we see the following:

	RecordID	Symptom 01	Symptom 02	Symptom 03	Symptom 04	Symptom 05	Symptom 06	Symptom 07	Symptom 08	Symptom 09	Symptom 10	PatientT otalTime	PhysicianT otalTime	CaregiverT otalTime	Initiator	PatientDi agnosis	NoPatient Questions	PatientQu estionsM eds	Patient ellness
2	2	Ringing in	Cognitive	Occurs dai	Facial flush	Nasal cong	Nasal cong	Depression	Fatigue	Sensitivity	Aneurysms	9	7	22	Physician	YES	1	NO	NO
3	3	Heightene	Eye-strain	Sleep Apne	Anorexia c	Weakness	Brain trum	Occurs dai	Constant-	Can occur	Bleeding ir	4	-2	27	Caregiver	NO	5	YES	YES
4	4	Head pain	Depression	Sinus infec	Indigestior	Pain felt o	Diet and fl	Sinus infec	Food cravi	Dull achy p	Depression	30	-16	27	Patient	NO	2	NO	YES
5	5	Nausea qu	Can occur	Food cravi	Neck or ja	Muscle pai	Aneurysms	Occurs at	Vertigo an	Can occur	Sleep Apne	17	7	-2	Patient	NO	27	YES	NO
6	6	Eye proble	Runny eye	Cognitive	Brain trum	Anxiety	Poor conc	Eye-strain	Teeth grin	Light sensi	Allergies	13	12	8	Patient	YES	8	YES	NO
7	7	Can occur	Changes in	Stuffy or r	Muscle pai	Can occur	Changes in	Stuffy or r	Allergies	Heightene	Palpitatior	10	14	-2	Caregiver	YES	13	YES	NO
8	8	Food cravi	Stabbing p	Anorexia c	Eye proble	Visual disti	Tight press	Sound sen	Droopy ey	Vertigo an	Neck or ja	2	3	5	Caregiver	NO	20	YES	YES
9	9	Head pain	Cognitive	Depression	Nasal cong	Poor postu	Poor conc	Head pain	Shortness	Diet and fl	Droopy ey	18	-16	19	Physician	YES	6	NO	YES
10	10	Dental pro	Pain in the	Diet and fl	Nasal cong	Aneurysms	Sleep Apne	Head pain	Tight press	Changes in	Runny eye	3	18	-1	Physician	NO	2	YES	NO
11	11	Sound sen	Ringing in	Eye proble	Head pain	Constant-	Sound sen	Anxiety	Fatigue	Droopy ey	Head pain	20	-1	8	Physician	NO	4	NO	YES
12	12	Food cravi	Visual disti	Brain trum	Sinus infec	Visual disti	Dull achy p	Anxiety	Depression	Bleeding ir	Neck or ja	13	4	12	Physician	NO	2	YES	NO
13	13	Vertigo an	Excess caf	Pain in the	Pain felt o	Anorexia c	Neck injuri	Ringing in	Pain felt o	Nasal cong	Numbness	1	13	3	Patient	NO	9	NO	NO
14	14	Can occur	Poor postu	Neck injuri	Constant-	Nasal cong	Nausea qu	Stuffy or r	Runny eye	Runny eye	Pain felt o	14	6	13	Patient	YES	3	YES	YES
15	15	Stress	Occurs at	Anxiety	Depression	Visual disti	Teeth grin	Excess caf	Numbness	Insomnia	Nausea qu	9	18	-11	Physician	YES	10	NO	YES

Part of dialog data file

Plenty of interesting data! The next step would be to load it into Watson Analytics, but first, let's peek at what we find in the patient history section of our data. The following screenshot shows what we find:

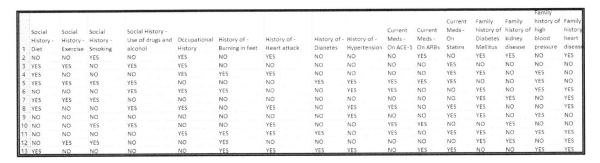

Patient history section

Without spending too much time looking at the raw data, let's proceed to load the data into Watson Analytics.

Reviewing the results

Once the data has been loaded, we can get to know it a bit. One way of doing this is to create a prediction on our file, but starting with a new analysis, using the following steps:

1. Click on **Predict** and select our file. On the **Create a new analysis** page, you can click on the link that says **Edit this workbook's field properties**, as shown in the following screenshot:

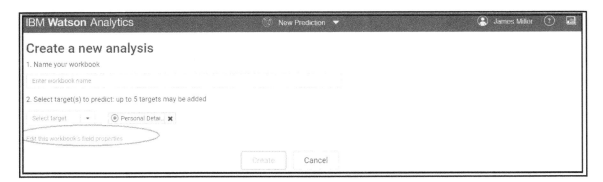

2. Once you click on the link, you will see the **Field Properties** page, as shown in the following screenshot:

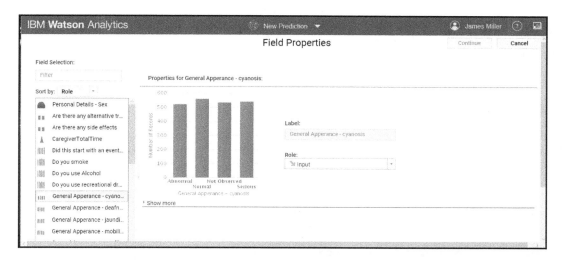

3. On this page, every column found in the file is listed down the left-hand side of the page. Clicking on the column selects it and allows you to see the name of the column, the label being used for the column, its role, and its measurement level.

The **Label** function maps a value in the data to a phrase that is a better description of the value. The **Role** function determines how a field is used (in a prediction), and measurement levels can be changed to improve the accuracy of your prediction.

Although we won't actually change anything at this time, scrolling through the data columns in this way is an easy way to get to know our data file. Scrolling through this list, we can see some interesting data columns, including those associated with patient history, listed as follows:

- **Number of illnesses**
- **Number of hospital stays**
- **Number of surgeries**

I would think that it would be of value to determine whether there is anything within the dialog data that may drive up the number of illnesses, hospital stays, and/or surgeries for patients. In other words, can we use Watson Analytics to *find a pattern* within our data that can be used to predict an outcome?

Going further, we can identify some **prediction targets**, such as the number of illness, (hospital) stays, and surgeries. However, at the moment, we don't know how to identify one or more **predictive drivers** within our dialog data. One option could be the patients' responses to questions such as *Do you smoke?* or *Do you use recreational drugs?*, or perhaps more emphasis should be on *dialog statistics*, such as the (total) length of time that the physician speaks during the dialog (or the length of time that the patient speaks).

Exploring the dialog data

So, if you are not sure of the next steps that you should take, you can use the Watson Analytics **Explore** function to keep moving forward. As a reminder, you can use **Explore** to develop questions to ask about the data (and identify some possible predictive drivers).

So, from the **Welcome** page, we can click **Explore** and select our data. Watson Analytics asks us **What do you want to explore in "Dialog_Info"?** and then lists a number of possible questions, as shown in the following screenshot:

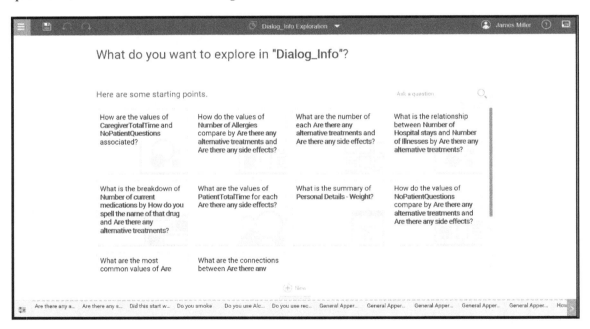

Rather than use one of Watson's suggestions, let's think. Can we simply ask Watson **What drives the number of illnesses**? Yes, we can. If we type this into the search bar (as shown in the following screenshot), Watson provides some possible predicted questions:

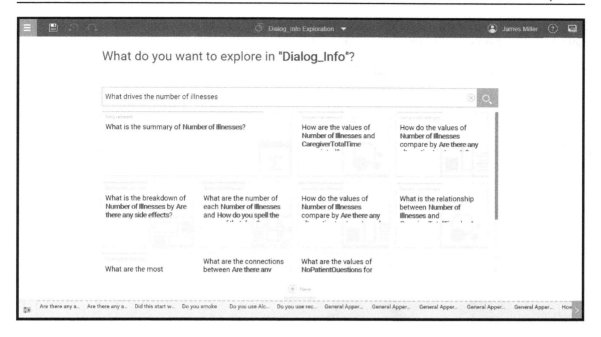

Some of the predicted questions are quite helpful, driving more thought on our part, such as **What is the summary of Number of Illness?** and **How are the values of Number of Illnesses and CaregiverTotalTime associated**?. Just reading through these prompts sparks more thoughts and questions that we could ask Watson, but for now, let's do some more exploring by clicking on some of the prompts. If we start with the summary question (**What is the summary of Number of Illnesses**), then we may not be too impressed, as you might guess from looking at the following screenshot:

But across the top of the page, there is a band of useful information that is based upon our selection, as shown in the following screenshot:

A good example is **How do the values of Number of Illnesses compare by Do you use recreational drugs**? Clicking on that image will open up the details, as shown in the following screenshot:

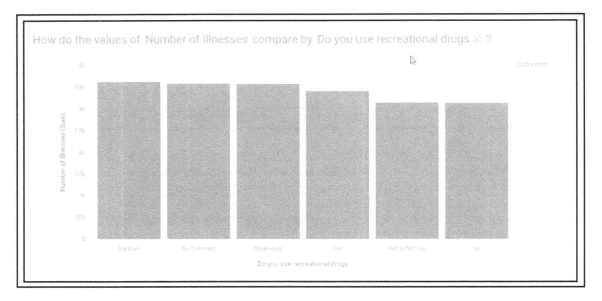

From this visualization, we can see a slight increase in the number of illnesses for patients that admit to medium or moderate recreational drug use (one might also presume that the answer **No Comment** might also implies similar drug use!).

Collecting the data

This is an interesting observation, and might be good to save so that we can come back to it later. IBM Watson Analytics lets you set aside or collect interesting or important visualizations from your data explorations. These collected assets can then be added to dashboards and stories that you can create later in **Assemble** (we will go over this later in the chapter).

First, some notes on collections:

- The visualizations you collect during an exploration remain interactive. This means that when you add them to a dashboard or story, you can still work with the live data.
- You can still make modifications to the data that's displayed in the visualization in **Assemble** (in the same way that you can edit it in **Explore**).
- You can enhance the visualization in **Assemble** by tweaking the settings that are applied to the exploration (but only when it is in **Assemble**), such as the grid lines, marker shapes, line styles, colors, and palettes.
- If you collect multiple visualizations, then when you come to use them in **Assemble**, you can save time by selecting them all at once and editing the properties that are common to all of the selected visualizations.

You can add a filter to a collected visualization in **Assemble**. Filters that are added in **Assemble** do not apply to the visualization in **Explore**. To add this visualization to your collection (as you might do from time to time as you work on Watson Analytics), take the following steps:

1. Click the **Collect** icon at the bottom left of the page, as shown in the following screenshot:

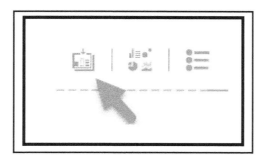

2. After you start collecting, you can use the **Collection** to view, track, and manage your collected assets. You access the collection view by clicking on the **Collection** icon located in the upper right of the Watson Analytics page, as shown in the following screenshot:

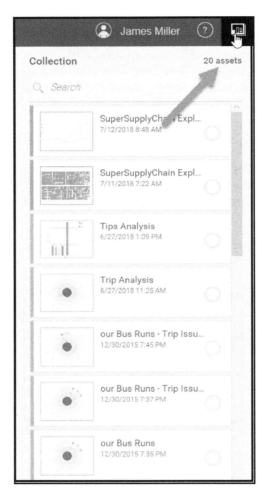

The **Collection** displays a list of thumbnail images that represent the items that you have collected over time.

Moving on

Now, let's quickly click on the field named **Do you use recreational drugs** in the visualization and change it to one of our other suspected prediction drivers: **Do you smoke**. The following screenshot shows you how to do this:

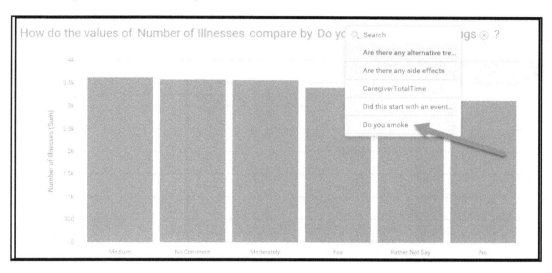

Another, perhaps more curious, visualization will be presented to us, as shown in the following screenshot:

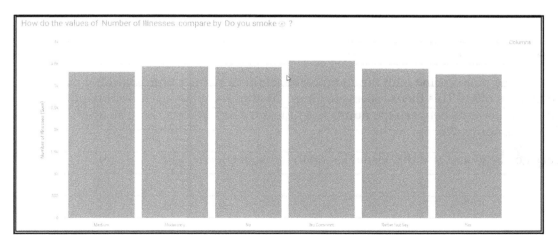

There doesn't seem to be any material difference in the number of illnesses recorded for those who smoke and those who do not. Either way, let's go ahead and add this visualization to our collection (by clicking the **Collect** icon at the bottom left of the page, as we did for the previous visualization).

Now, at this point, another interesting thought will occur to us: What about the patient's response to the question of alcohol use? If we change the column name again, we will see the following visualization:

This seems more in-line with the common belief that a regular user of alcohol might indeed be ill more often. This theory seems to jump out at us from the visualization quite quickly, given the contrast between the number of illnesses displayed for those answering **Yes** and those answering **No**.

Let's go ahead and add this visualization to our collection as well.

Recap

So, let's take a minute to look over what we just did:

1. We received a file of data that contained the results of patient dialogs, along with some pertinent patient history.

2. We looked at some of the data and then went ahead and loaded it into Watson Analytics.

3. Anxious to create a prediction of our data, we started by creating a **New Prediction**, but rather than completing it, we used the **Field Properties** feature to scroll through the columns of data so that we could obtain an understanding of what we had to work with.

4. At this point, we determined that we didn't know enough to move forward, so we used the IBM Watson Analytics **Explore** feature to dive deeper into the data.

5. From there, we were able to build upon Watson's prompts and establish a target for our prediction of **Number of Illnesses**. We also found some interesting insights into the data, such as the fact that the use of recreational drugs as well as smoking seems to not materially affect the number of illnesses for a patient, but the use of alcohol does.

6. We were able to glean these insights from the data quickly via Watson Analytics's generated visualizations. Since these seem key, we saved each of these visualizations as assets to our collection.

7. At this point, we know our data pretty well, and we have some solid ideas in mind of what might drive or affect our prediction, so now it's time to create our prediction.

8. If we click on the file's tile from the Watson Analytics **Welcome** page, Watson again gives us some starting points. Since we think we have a good idea as to how to proceed with our prediction, we can just click on the **Predict** icon at the bottom of the dialog, as shown in the following screenshot:

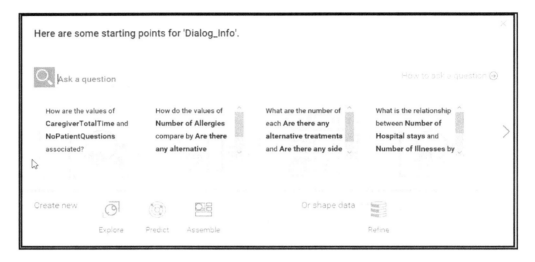

9. Watson will then present the **Create a new analysis** page, as shown in the following screenshot:

10. We can fill in a name and select the target that we are interested in (such as **Number of Illnesses**), as shown in the following screenshot:

11. Finally, we can click on the button labeled **Create,** and Watson Analytics will begin its analysis of our data, as shown in the following screenshot:

Results

The following screenshot shows our Watson Analytics prediction based upon our selected target:

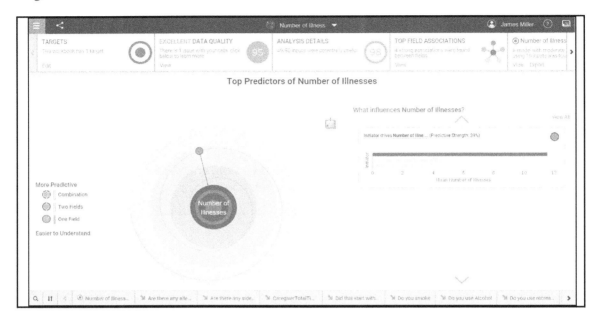

Watson Analytics prediction

We can see that Watson Analytics has performed its analysis and has determined that the number of illnesses is driven by the **Initiator** field. This can be clearly seen by examining the gray bullseye, as shown in the following screenshot:

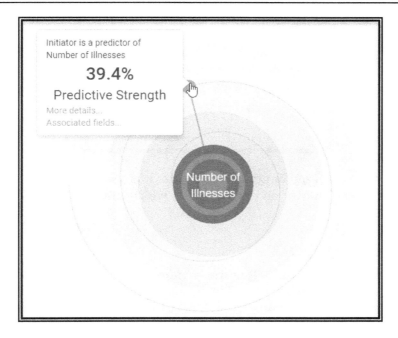

The blue dot (the only dot) shows us that **Initiator** is a predictor of **Number of Illness**, with a **Predictive Strength** of 39.4%. Predictive strength is the measurement used to show the importance of a field in relationship to its ability to help predict an outcome. The higher the predictive strength, the stronger the correlation with what is being predicted.

Data quality of the prediction

Data quality is the degree to which data is suitable for analysis. Before we proceed any further with our project, we need to know what the quality of our data is. Well, fortunately IBM Watson Analytics provides some help with this, starting with its data quality score. This is referred to as a shorthand representation of Watson's assessment of the quality of our data. The score is measured on a scale of 0–100, with 100 representing the highest possible quality of data.

Across the top of our prediction, we can see a variety of analysis results, including the data quality score, as shown in the following screenshot:

Watson Analytics has analyzed our data and awarded us a score of 95, which is an excellent score. To see more, you can click on the **View** link, which shows the

Data quality report

The Watson Analytics **Data Quality Report** provides graphical and textual information about the data quality of the data that has been analyzed. The report provides information on the data as a whole, as well as on each individual column of data, as shown in the following screenshot:

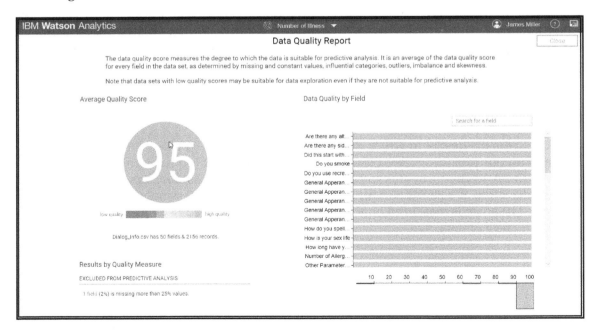

Data quality report

If the data quality by field is not shown, you can click on the overall data quality score to see the distribution of quality scores for all of the individual columns of data within your data file.

More predictive strength

Back on the main prediction page, Watson Analytics shows what is named the prediction scenario selector (shown in the following screenshot). This lets you drill deeper into the insights that may be hidden in the data. With the prediction scenario selector, you can specify how many fields you want to view that act as predictors for your target (other than the **Initiator** in our example):

If we click on **Two Fields**, Watson Analytics changes our visualization and we see a new set of visualizations, as shown in the following screenshot. We can now see how these two variables influence the number of illnesses (our target):

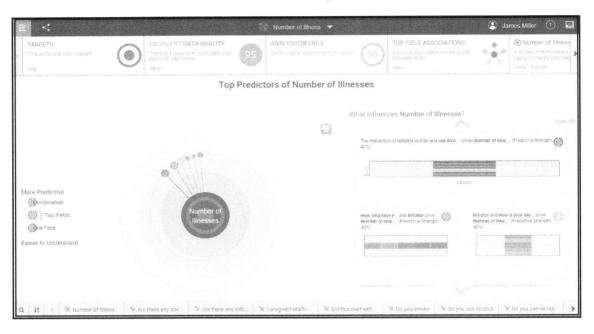

Results reflecting the top predictors of number of illnesses

There are now three colored dots on our bullseye. If we click on each of the three new dots, we will see that the following pattern was found in our data:

More interesting details. According to Watson Analytics, other than who initiated the dialog between the physician and the patient, the following topics of discussion have an impact on the patient's overall heath:

- The patient's use of alcohol
- How long a patient has had symptoms
- How the patient views their sex life

As a data scientist, you should investigate the prediction scenario selector. For example, if you select **Combination**, the visualizations provide a deeper and perhaps more predictive analysis of the data by showing how a combination of variables influences your target. Choosing **One Field** leads to predictions that are easier to understand, but that might be less predictive. Choosing **Combination** might lead to a prediction that is more accurate, but harder to understand. Choosing **Two Fields** might give you predictions that are somewhere in the middle.

More detail

If we go back to the **One Field** predictor, we can see again that Watson has provided our predictor with a corresponding snapshot visualization that contains information about the predictor and how it affects the target. The color of the circle in the spiral visualization is also found in the corresponding detailed visualization. In our prediction, the blue circle in the spiral visualization for the **Initiator** predictor is included in the corresponding detailed visualization for the **Initiator**, as shown in the following screenshot:

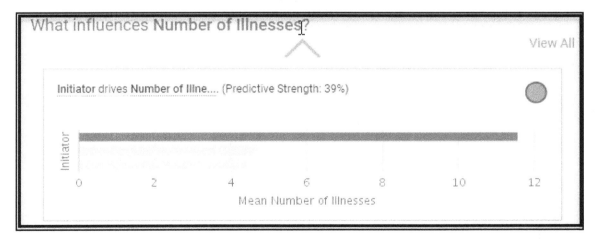

You can click on the visualization to see it in more detail on the **Main Insight** page. The **Main Insight** page for the **Initiator** is shown in the following screenshot:

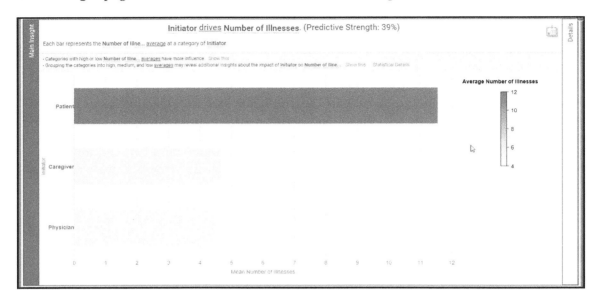

Main Insight page for the Initiator

You can examine the *top* insights that were derived by Watson Analytics in its analysis. You can then go to the **Details** page to drill further into the details for the individual fields and interactions. Both pages provide links to change the display and provide additional details, which might reveal some points of interest that could be useful for further investigations.

For example, on the **Details** page, we might see the following statement:

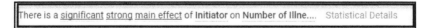

We might also see the following **Statistical Details**:

Statistical Details

ANOVA Table

Source	Sum of Squares	df	Mean Square	F	Sig.
Initiator	22,054.10	2	11,027.05	699.85	.00
Error	33,923.50	2,153	15.76		
Total	55,977.60	2,155			

Predictive Strength (1-Relative Error) = 39%
Effect Size (Eta-square): .39
The F is statistically significant, so reject the null hypothesis that the Number of Illnesses means are equal across the categories of Initiator.

Assembling a story

Now is the time to assemble the story that we want to tell. This is done by presenting the analyses and insights that we collected using **Explore** and **Predict** earlier in this chapter, as well as perhaps some new visualizations, text, images, and shapes, or perhaps other media. To do this, let's go through the following steps:

As we have already mentioned (and you will find this over and over throughout the Watson Analytics documentation), you should be sure to make it a habit, while in **Explore**, **Predict**, and **Assemble**, to save key visualizations by adding them to your collection. That way, when you assemble a story, you can access your collection and simply drag items into your story!

1. To build our story, click on **Assemble** on the main Watson Analytics **Welcome** page, as shown in the following screenshot:

2. If we weren't sure what data we were going to use in our story, we could scroll through the list of data files and click on an appropriate file to select it. In our story, we know that we want to use the patient dialog data that we have been working on, so we can just click on the button labeled **Skip**. Watson displays the **Create** page, as shown in the following screenshot:

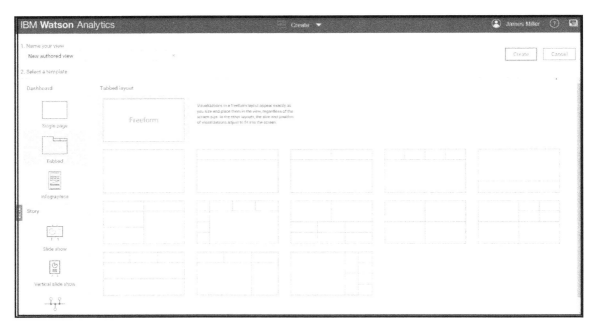

Create page

3. If we selected a dataset (rather than **Skip**), then the name of the view defaults to the name of that dataset. We didn't select a data file, so we need to change the name of your view by typing the new name in the **Name your view** field.

4. Under the **Story** caption, (see the left-hand side of the page), we now need to select one of the story types. These are **Slide show** (which tells your story through a series of slides, similar to a Microsoft PowerPoint presentation), **Vertical slide show** (which is a slide show in which you move through the slides vertically), or **Time journey** (which tells your story over time, where the slides in the story are in a precise sequence that is related to a time frame; this type of story can be used to emphasize that the analysis is related to time).

5. Next, under **Select a template**, click on the layout that you want to use for the story. We'll use **Freeform**. Finally, click on the button labeled **Create**. The view will be saved and the scene selector (at the bottom of the page) contains one empty scene, as shown in the following screenshot:

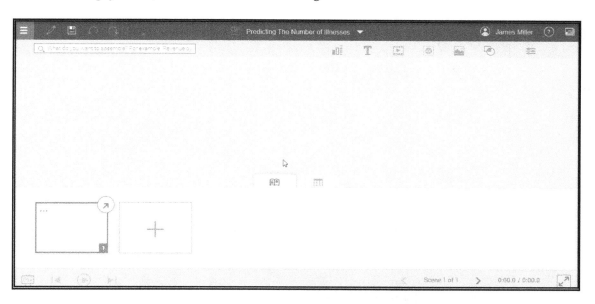

Now, we are ready to add our items or assets to the story slides. You can add items and visualizations in a variety of ways, but let's start by reusing some of our saved visualizations (those we saved into our collection).

6. We click the **Collections** icon (in the upper-right corner of the main toolbar) and then drag and drop the selected visualization from the collection, as shown in the following screenshot:

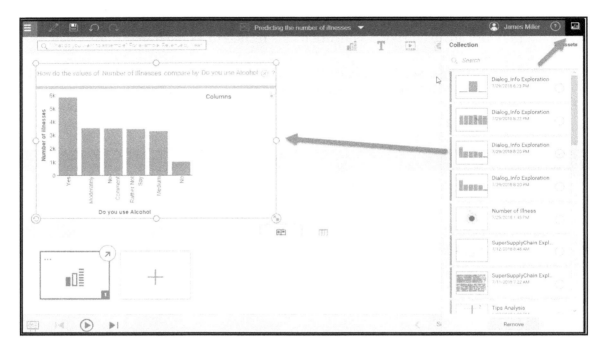

7. To add a title to our slide, click on the **...** and then click on the pencil icon. In the **Rename this scene** popup (shown in the following screenshot), you can provide a meaningful name for the current slide (or scene):

8. You can add text, media, web pages, images, and shapes to any of your story slides simply by clicking the particular icon. Let's just add some text to this first story slide to explain the visualization a bit more. To do that, we click on the text icon (the **T** icon), and Watson Analytics will add a text box for you to type what you want (as shown in the following screenshot):

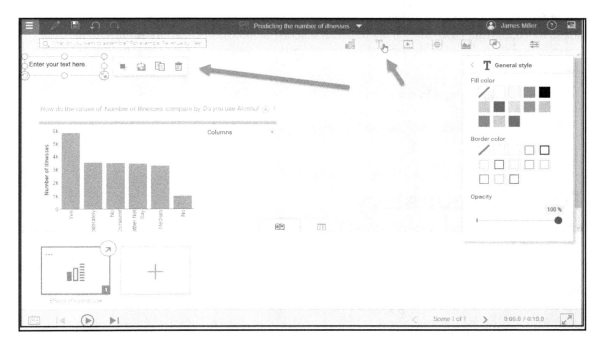

9. Once we have completed this slide, or scene, we can add another scene to the story by clicking the + icon (as shown in the following screenshot), selecting a template, and then clicking **USE**:

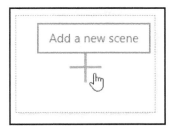

We can repeat the preceding process to add another saved visualization to the story from our collection. This time, we'll add the visualization showing the affect of the **Initiator** on the number of patient illnesses.

While you work on creating and editing your IBM Watson Analytics story, you can experiment with the easy ways in which you can mange the story. For example, to move an object from one scene to another, you can just drag the object to the new scene in the scene selector. To change the order of scenes in the scene selector, you can again just drag a selected scene to the new desired position. Finally, to delete a scene, click on the ... and then click on the trash can icon.

 Building a Watson Analytics story is very similar to creating a Microsoft PowerPoint slide deck presentation, with a story as a slide deck and the scenes as the slides.

Testing your story

After you've assembled a story in IBM Watson Analytics, it is a good idea to test it to see how it will look to someone who is viewing it. You will also want to ensure that the visualizations appear and disappear at the correct time during the scene.

Again, this is very similar to how you would construct a Microsoft PowerPoint slide deck and test it before an upcoming presentation.

To test your story, you simply do the following:

1. Make sure that it is saved by clicking on the save icon:

2. Exit **Design** or **Change** mode by clicking on the pencil icon:

3. Switch to full screen by tapping the **Screen** mode icon:

4. Use the video controls to move forward and backward through the story:

In the next chapter's project, we will cover how to build stories in much more detail, but for now, you should have a good understanding of the process.

Summary

In this chapter, we introduced the idea of blending patient history data with data sourced from dialogs between a physician and a patient. We then went through the process that is required to create an IBM Watson Analytics project so that you can use Watson to gain a better understanding of the provided data, establish a project objective, use Watson Analytics to create a prediction based upon the data, and finally construct a Watson story to share the insights that you gained.

In the next chapter, you will learn about sentiment analysis, using Watson Analytics to automatically analyze and categorize text posted to social media in an attempt to determine an audience's feeling about a topic.

Social Media Sentiment Analysis

5

In this chapter, we will learn about sentiment analysis: using Watson Analytics to automatically analyze and categorize text posted to social media, in an attempt to determine an audience's feelings about a topic.

As with our previous chapters, the breakdown for this chapter will be as follows:

- The problem defined
- Getting started
- Building the project
- Reviewing the results

The problem defined

Sentiment analysis, or mining for opinions – when we perform this type of project, multiple technologies can be leveraged, for example **Natural Language Processing** (**NLP**), textual analysis, and computational linguistics, to identify and extract subjective material from a source. Sentiment analysis is and has been used in a variety of ways, and more opportunities appear every day. One interesting example is that it is used by political candidates and administrations in an attempt to monitor overall opinions about policy changes and campaign announcements, empowering them to fine-tune their approach and messaging to better relate to voters and constituents.

To further drive the point, in a recent blog posting, *Mike Waldron*, Head of Marketing and Sales at AYLIEN , said the following:

> *"As more and more content is created and shared online, through social channels, blogs, review sites and so on, we are becoming more and more vocal and open about our experiences online. In a recent study carried out by Zendesk, it was noted that 45% of people share bad customer service experiences and 30% share good customer service experiences via social media* (`https://www.zendesk.com/resources/customer-service-and-lifetime-customer-value/`)*", which again highlights" the need and desire for businesses to mine this information to gain business insight from it has also increased."*

Social media and IBM Watson Analytics

IBM Watson Analytics for Social Media is a fairly new offering in Watson Analytics and is designed to help you analyze content in social media posts, even those that are in Arabic, French, German, Italian, Portuguese, or Spanish.

As with all of Watson Analytics, Watson Analytics for Social Media aims to discover insights; this feature mines conversations in social media that are found to be related to your interest, with the intent of answering questions such as the following (listed in the product documentation):

- What are customers hearing and saying about my brand?
- What are the most talked about product qualities in my product grouping?
- Are reactions respectable, good, or not so much?
- What is the opposition doing for market stimulation?
- Is my employer's reputation affecting my capability to recruit the highest talent?
- What are the reputations of the new sellers that I may be considering?
- What issues are most significant for my community?

To become familiar with this feature, in this chapter we will create a Watson Analytics project in an attempt to analyze and understand a topic of interest by specifying certain topics and keywords, as well as by using various pertinent Watson Analytics-produced ideas around keywords.

Let's get started!

Getting started

There is a process to follow to use Watson Analytics for Social Media. The process is referred to as the social media workflow. It is similar to the process (or workflow) that should be followed for any Watson Analytics project. The workflow is as follows:

1. Create a Watson Analytics project
2. Identify or create a data source (or dataset)
3. View the Watson Analytics-generated visualizations

Creating a Watson Analytics social media project

For social media projects, the particulars of this workflow process look like this:

- **Specify topics to analyze**: You specify the keywords to include, plus you can also exclude keywords and define context keywords. Use suggestions that we provide to get more ideas about keywords.
- **Specify the date range**: By default, the last four weeks are searched and analyzed.
- **Specify the types of sources that you want to retrieve documents from**: Sources that are available include forums, reviews, Facebook pages, Reddit pages, video descriptions and comments, blogs, and news.
- **Review the suggestions for your topics, because new suggestions might appear after you specify the date range and sources**: Optionally, define themes to provide more clarity in the analysis.
- **Identify or create a dataset to retrieve documents that match the criteria that you specified**: Watson Analytics for Social Media retrieves the documents, analyzes them, creates visualizations, and creates a dataset. View the visualizations that Watson Analytics for Social Media creates for you.

In this chapter, we will assume that a not-for-profit organization is interested in providing insights on the general sentiment of Amazon's customer service levels. Basically, what is being said about the Amazon customer service experience?

 If you aren't sure what Amazon is (really?), then Amazon is an American electronic commerce and cloud computing company based in Seattle, Washington that was founded by Jeff Bezos on July 5, 1994. The tech giant is the largest internet retailer in the world as measured by revenue and market capitalization, and second largest after the Alibaba Group in terms of total sales.

Building the project

As we've already stated, every Watson Analytics project that intends to analyze social media content must begin with defining a project as step one. Watson Analytics projects contain information about the topics and themes that you want to investigate. The project also covers the visual and text insights that are generated from the topics and themes you are interested in.

Depending on which version of IBM Watson Analytics for Social Media you are using (or your subscription level), the number and type of social media documents (such as Facebook and Reddit pages) that are supported varies. In addition, for YouTube content, Watson Analytics for Social Media can access up to 15 months of historical data. For all other content, 24 months of historical data can be accessed.

To control the volume of documents that is retrieved, carefully consider the topic keywords, context keywords, and exclude keywords that you specify. Also, check what time frame, sources, and languages provide the best results for the analysis that you want to do. Social media datasets contribute to your data limit in IBM Watson Analytics.

The entire content of social media documents that match the criteria that you establish is retrieved and analyzed. Information about mentions of your keywords in the documents that are retrieved is contained in your dataset and is represented in the visualizations on the **Analysis** tab.

To get started, in Watson Analytics click the arrow at the far left on the app bar, then click on **IBM Watson Analytics for Social Media**.

Note: depending on your version of Watson Analytics, access to social media might be slightly different.

The following screenshot shows the **IBM Watson Analytics for Social Media Welcome** page:

IBM Watson Analytics for Social Media Welcome page

Project creation step by step

First, click on the **New project** icon, then on the **Create a new social media project** tab, and enter a name for the social media project:

Create a new social media project tab

Next, we can click on the button labeled **Next**. A new Watson Analytics Social Media project is then created for us, which you can now access from the main page of Watson Analytics for Social Media.

Adding topics

Take a look at the following screenshot:

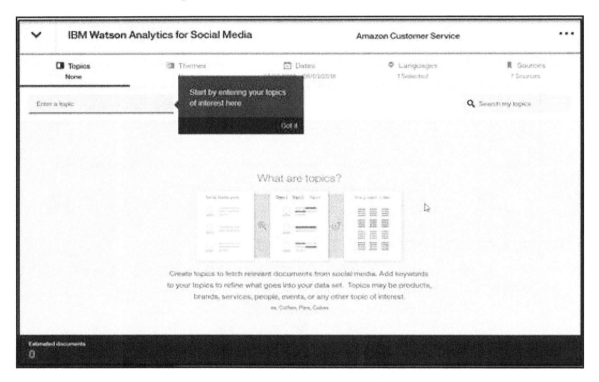

Adding topics

To add topics to our social media project, we can type them in the **Enter a topic** text area and then click the **Add** button, as shown in the following screenshot:

Adding Amazon Customer service topic

A topic embodies a portion of content from social media that you want to retrieve and examine (for example, brands, products, services, or events). You can enter as many topics as you want, but you need to add each topic separately. You can always click on a topic to edit it later. Take a look at the following screenshot:

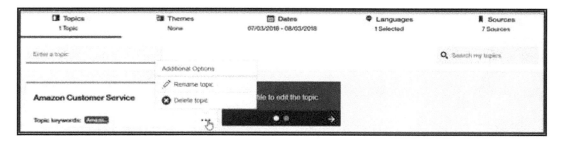

Adding each topic separately

Additionally, when you click on one of your entered topics, you can create topic keywords, context keywords, and exclusion keywords for each topic.

 Currently, all of the keywords entered and used must be in Arabic, Chinese, English, French, German, Italian, Portuguese, Russian, or Spanish.

Take a look at the following screenshot:

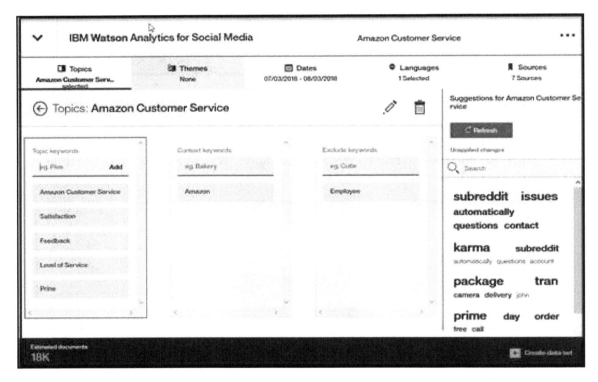

Creating topic keywords, context keywords, and exclusion keywords for each topic.

The name of the topic is always created as a topic keyword. At least one topic keyword must be present for social media content to be retrieved. Consider adding alternative versions of the topic to ensure the most complete retrieval of data. Watson Analytics for Social Media provides topic and keyword suggestions in the **Suggestions** pane to help you determine other keywords that you might want to include in your project. After entering or changing topics and keywords, you should always click on the **Suggestion** pane and the **Refresh** button to view an updated list of alternative entries, based upon your most current entries.

Social media investigative themes

As an option, you can also click on **Themes** to create investigative themes that consist of an attribute or list of attributes on which you want to break down an entered topic, as shown in the following screenshot:

Selecting themes

Example: We can use theme attributes in our project, which include availability, loyalty, quality, and service. You add themes in the same way as you add topics. Each theme applies to all of your entered topics. In topics, you can enter as many themes as you want although again you must add each theme individually. You can also click on **Themes** to add theme keywords and, optionally, context keyword, and exclude keywords that apply to that theme (just like your topics). Theme keywords must also be in Arabic, Chinese, English, French, German, Italian, Portuguese, Russian, or Spanish. Take a look at the following screenshot:

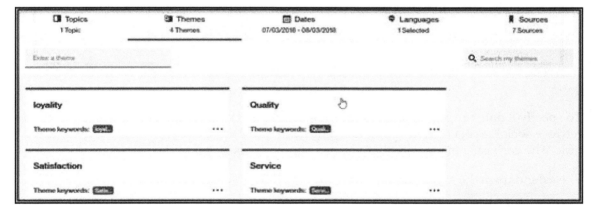

Theme attributes

Adding dates

Just like with any data query, it is always a good idea to try and limit the amount of data to retrieve and process. In Watson Analytics for Social Media, to accomplish this you can use the date range, as shown in the following screenshot:

Using date range

To specify a date range, you can click on **Dates** and specify the time period that you want to retrieve social media content from. The dates and times are inclusive and are in your local time. The earliest starting date that you can choose is restricted in the **Start date** calendar.

The calendars make it easy to set a start and end date. I've used January 1st to August 3rd:

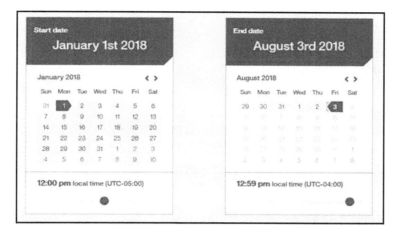

Calendar displaying start and end dates

Languages

You can select which languages you want to include in your project by clicking the **Languages** tab. For various reasons, such as cultural differences, it is important to carefully determine which languages are appropriate for your particular interest. In our project, I've left English by default as the only language to include:

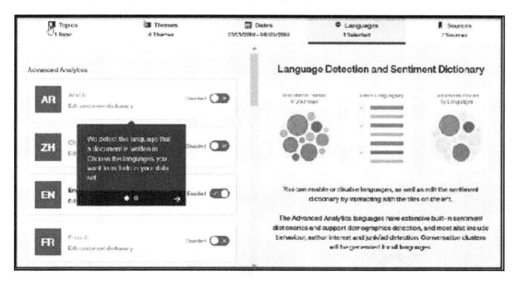

Selecting language

Sources

Finally, Watson Analytics for Social Media can collect from a number of media sources and you have the ability to determine which of the supported types you want to include and use in your project.

The currently supported media types are:

Forums	Retrieves from message boards and forums
Reviews	Retrieves comments and reviews from review sites
Facebook pages	Retrieves from many Facebook pages of top industries. Data is available from January 27, 2016 onward
Reddit pages	Retrieves from many Reddit pages
Videos	Retrieves video descriptions and comments posted to video sites
Blogs	Retrieves blog posts and their comments
News	Retrieves postings from major news websites and news wires

Clicking on **Sources** allows you the ability to turn any supported media type on or off, as shown in the following screenshot:

Turn any supported media type on or off

Once you are happy with your project setup and are ready to retrieve social media content (based upon the previously selected settings) and view visualizations about your topics and themes, you can click on the **Create dataset** icon, as shown in the following screenshot:

Create data set icon

You'll need to keep a few things in mind; the more sources you choose to include, and the broader the topic of focus:

- The longer it will take to retrieve the content
- The more space it will consume in your Watson Analytics environment

Processing time may not be a huge deterrent; however, the space required to process and store the results may be. Depending upon your subscription or version of Watson Analytics for Social Media, you may exceed your limits or potentially incur additional fees. To address these concerns, you can always reset your project selections to reduce the number of sources, or attempt to fine-tune or narrow your topic of interest by adding additional topics and/or keywords.

Reviewing the results

Once you click the **Create dataset** icon, Watson Analytics for Social Media will provide an estimate of the resources the project will consume and allow you to go **Back** or **Continue**:

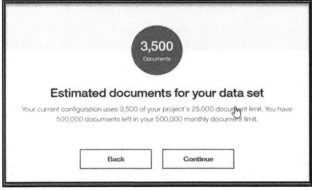

Watson Analytics providing an estimate of the resources

If you **Continue**, Watson Analytics for Social Media will provide an analysis progress status, as shown in the following screenshot:

Analysis progress

And when the analysis is completed, you will see the completed message, as well as a count of the total documents and total mentions that the analysis resulted from in the **Analysis** tab, as shown in the following screenshot:

Complete analysis displayed

Once the analysis is complete, we can click on the **View Analysis** icon (in the bottom middle of the **Analysis** tab) to view our projects results, as shown in the following screenshot:

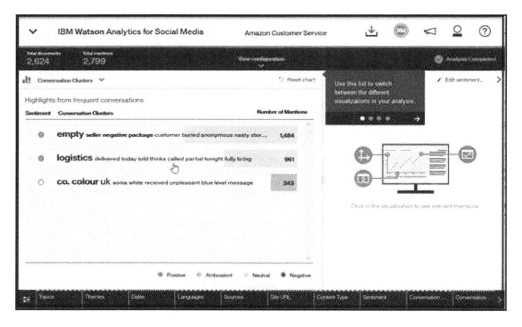

Viewing the analysis

Watson Analytics for Social Media automatically generates visualizations as part of the project analysis results. You can interact with those visualizations to do things such as filtering, either individually (right-click a part of the visualization and click the **Exclude** button), or all at once (click a column heading in the data tray and select all of the items you want to filter on).

Deeper dive – conversation clusters

Watson Analytics features conversation cluster visualizations that can be used to comprehend important terms that appear in social media posts about the topics you added as part of your project. This helps you to find trends and will point out facets and insights that you may not have been thinking of back when you were defining your project topics and themes. Take a look at the following screenshot:

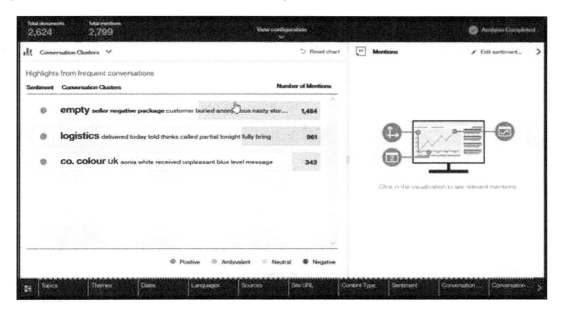

Defining your project topics and themes

Each distinct conversation cluster will show terms that appear together in a noteworthy amount of social media content. If a term is found often, it will be shown using a heavier font in the conversation cluster. In our project, we see the terms **empty**, **logistics,** and **co.colour uk**.

If you click on the **empty** term, Watson Analytics for Social Media shows the content and posts that contain the term in the panel on the right-hand side of the page. In addition, in some cases, if you click on the link to the selected content, you are sent to the actual content (where you can view the original post or mention), as shown in the following screenshot:

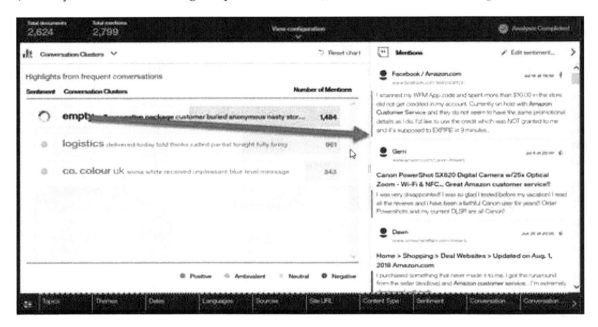

Empty term

Navigation

When you click on the **View Analysis** icon, the default view starts with **Conversation Clusters** already selected for you, as you saw in the preceding screenshot. Keep in mind that at any time you can easily click on the selected tab, then click to navigate to any of the project analysis result types grouped under **What**, **Where**, and **Who,** as shown in the following screenshot:

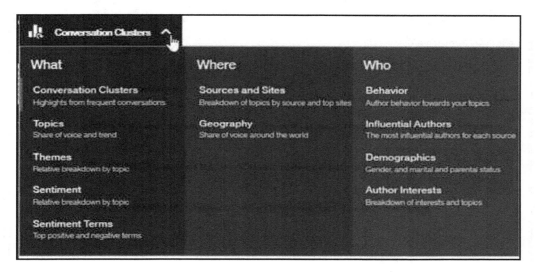

Default view

You can always switch back to the project configuration at any time by clicking the **View configuration** icon. This allows you to modify what you defined for your project. Take a look at the following screenshot:

View configuration icon

Topics

Topic visualization can be leveraged to find trends with them and share a voice for the topics that you have set. To view topics, you can click on **Conversation Clusters** and then select **Topics,** as shown in the following screenshot:

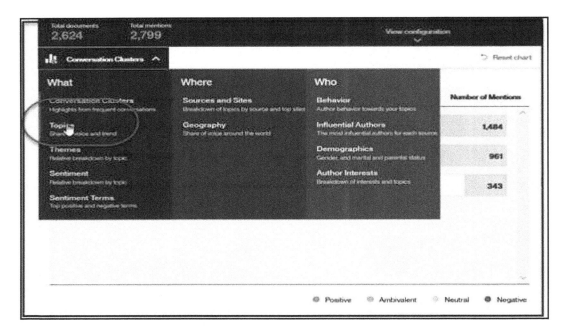

View topics- Click on Conversation Clusters

 Share of Voice in Online Advertising is an **ad revenue model that focuses on weight or percentage among other advertisers**. For example, if there are four advertisers on a website, each advertiser gets 25 percent of the advertising weight (en.wikipedia.org/wiki/Share_of_voice).

The following screenshot shows the **Topics** visualization from our project results. Basically, this graphic (the themes trend chart) shows us the mentions of our topic, Amazon customer service, by month throughout our selected date range:

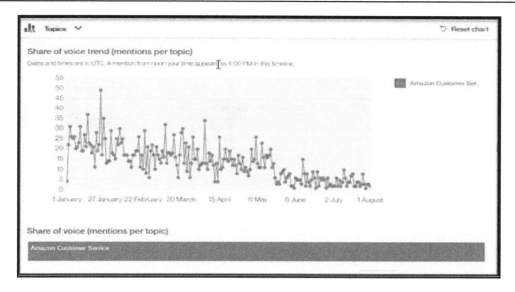

Topics visualization from our project results

If you click on any data point in the chart, Watson Analytics for Social Media loads the related content in the pane on the right of the page. It also underlines various keywords in the content relevant to the project analysis. In our project, we see that the phrases **can't get** and **very frustrated** are underlined for us in a corresponding post from www.facebook.com, as shown in the following screenshot:

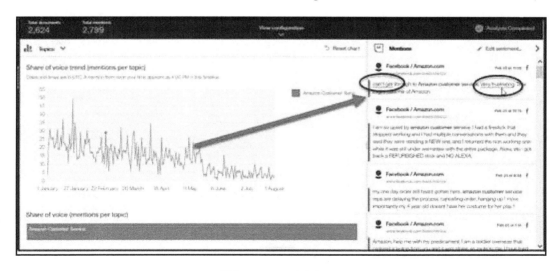

Clicking on any data point in the chart

In our project, since we are very interested in the topic of Amazon's customer service, the underlined phrases may pique some interest. If we click on the supplied link, we are conveniently transferred to the actual Facebook post. Take a look at the following screenshot:

Displaying the Facebook page

Another look

As we stated earlier in this chapter, the visualizations are pretty much interactive. Here is an example. If we again use the dropdown (now showing **Topics**) and select the **Themes** tab, as shown in the following screenshot:

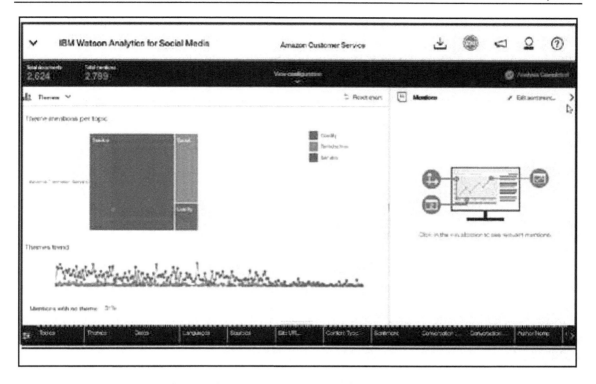

Select the Theme tab

The preceding screenshot is a visualization showing which themes are mentioned in the social media content found during the analysis. It also shows how these mentions break down by our different themes: Quality, Satisfaction, and Service.

We can filter a particular mention from our content (such as blanks). To do this, you can right-click a column in the visualization and click the **Exclude** button. In our project, we can filter by any of the themes, so let's try excluding **Service**. The following screenshot shows the updated graphic:

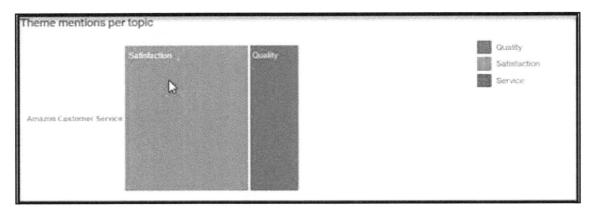

Updated graphic

Again, clicking on the graphic will show the content for the selected option mention in the right panel of the page:

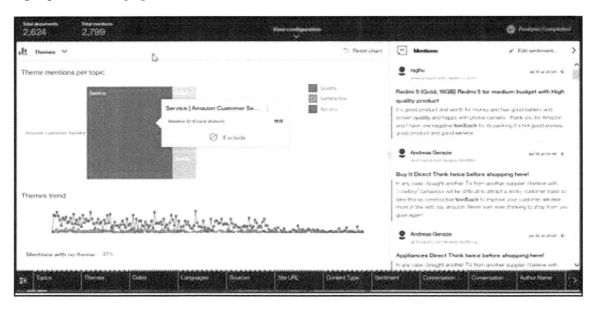

Graphic showing the content for the selected option

Sentiment

The sentiment visualization feature can be leveraged to gain an understanding of the tone of the social media content found during analysis. Sentiment is grouped by the topics that were specified when setting up the project. Relative sentiment shows the dispersion of constructive, undesirable, unbiased, and undecided sentiments. Sentiment terms are phrases that measure the feel of a mention. Sentiment shows whether a mention is good or bad. A mention is branded as undecided when it has the same number of good and bad sentiment phrases. A mention is branded as neutral when no sentiment terms are detected in it.

The sentiment trend chart illustrates the number of mentions by day, spanning the time range of our project, as shown in the following screenshot:

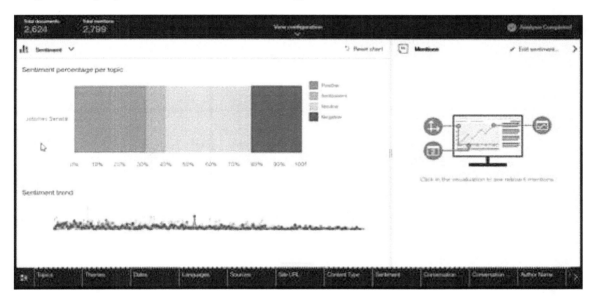

Sentiment trend chart

In our project, the visualization indicates to us that positive mentions are more common for social content mentioning Amazon customer service. This may be a bit clearer if we filter the visualization (right-click and select the **Exclude** button) by removing the neutral responses, as shown in the following screenshot:

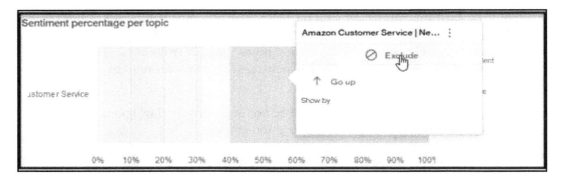

Selecting the Exclude button

Now the visualization is looking better:

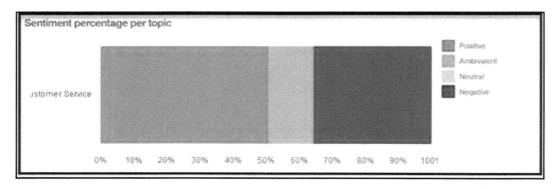

Sentiment percentage per topic visualization

Sentiment terms

Sentiment terms are phrases that measure the overall tone of a mention. Sentiment indicates whether a mention is good or bad. The sentiment phrase visualization can be used to refine a sentiment analysis dictionary. This page groups the terms into two groups: **Top positive** and **Top negative**. A neat feature is the ability for you again to click on a particular term that you may find interesting or most relevant and see its references in the right-hand side pane of the following screenshot:

Viewing neat features

In our project, we see that the top terms (for both positive and negative groups) are **satisfaction** and **NOT satisfaction**.

Geography

A geographical visualization is always a popular feature. In Watson Analytics for Social Media, you can use the geography visualization to inspect where social media documents have been posted.

Note from the product documentation: Geographic region is determined by the permanent location information in the author's profile and does not necessarily reflect the author's location when they created the document.

Geographical visualization

For our project, we see that most of our content sources are from North America, perhaps since Amazon headquarters is in the **United States**?

Sources and sites

The **Sources** and **Sites** visualization was designed to compare the different sources of your topics, then drilldown to see what sites had the most posts for that source. Sources that are available include forums, reviews, Facebook pages, Reddit pages, video descriptions and comments, blogs, and news. The sources shown in your visualization will be those that you selected as part of your project setup. Take a look at the following screenshot:

Sources and Sites visualization

In our project example, the generated visualization shows what sources have mentions based upon our project's configuration. Our selected sources were limited to reviews and Facebook pages. Again, you can get details about what sites had the most posts on the topic for a type of source by clicking on a source to drilldown on that source. Up to 15 sites with the most posts will appear in the generated visualization.

Influential authors

Random commentaries may be interesting, but interjections from those deemed more influential usually carry more weight. The Watson Analytics for Social Media influential authors visualization shows influential authors by source type. Influential authors are those on social media who are actively talking about the topics that we defined in our project. Take a look at the following screenshot:

Visualization showing influential authors

The influential author page, as shown in the preceding screenshot, displays your project's sources on the left-hand side (we selected **Reviews** and **Facebook pages**) and the authors in the middle of the page. The pane on the right-hand side of the page will show content if you click on a particular author.

You can see various author statistics, as well as two scores for each influential author when you hover over an author in the visualization, **Author engagement** and **Author influence**:

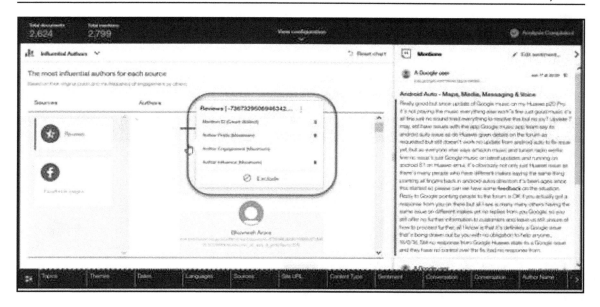

Author engagement and Author influence visualization

The author engagement score measures how much an author's posts on social media were engaged by other social media users. Author engagement is calculated by counting the number of times that other authors reacted to an author and the author's posts through comments, replies, and other reactions, depending on the source. There is no author engagement score for reviews and news sources. The author engagement scores for all authors are in the author engagement column in your project's corresponding dataset. The author influence score reflects how influential an author is in that specific social media source. The scores for all authors are in the author influence column in your project's corresponding dataset.

Author interests

The Watson Analytics for Social Media author interests visualization allows you to look a bit closer at the interest of the content authors. The visualization starts with the number of authors broken down by our topics, as shown in the following screenshot:

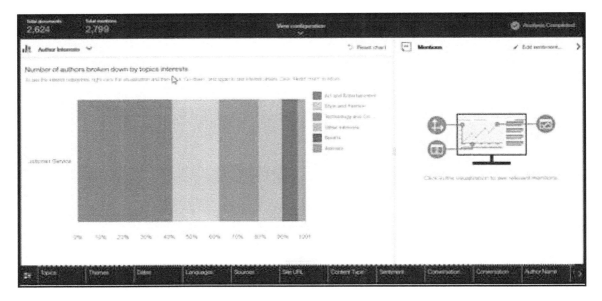

Visualization starting with the number of authors broken down by our topics

You can then drilldown two levels of detail here; by clicking on the context menu, you can filter the topics:

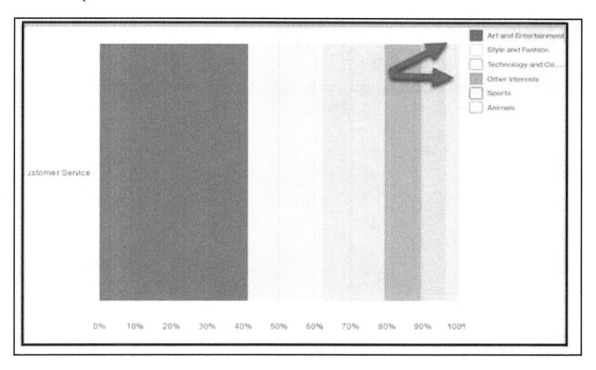

Filtering the topics

In our project, the preceding visualization shows the interest of the author Amazon customer service, categorized by various interests. We have selected only **Art and Entertainment** and **Other Interests**. Perhaps we want to drilldown further? What is **Other Interests** referring to? We can drilldown on this by right-clicking on the **Other Interest** button and then selecting the **Go down** button; then, you can see categories such as the **Games** and **Shopping** checkboxes:

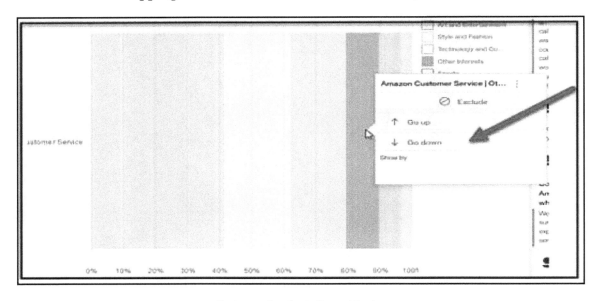

Viewing categories such as the Games and Shopping

Games and shopping

The following screenshot shows the **Games and Shopping** screen:

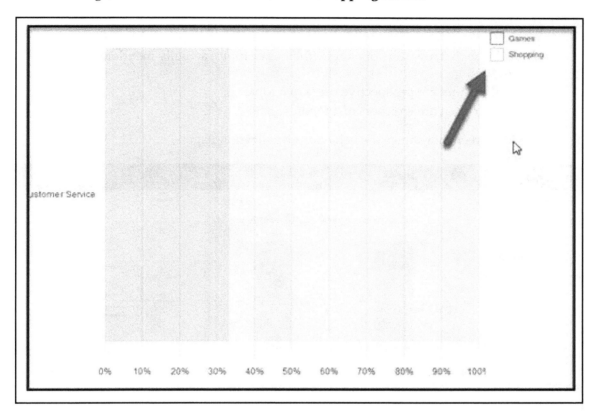

Games and shopping screen

Behavior

Moving on! Watson Analytics for Social Media analyzes text found in social media content in an attempt to determine the behavior of the authors. The behavior visualization shows the number of mentions by author in each of the following behavior categories:

- Authors that are users of a topic (themes or topics actually mentioned by authors)
- Authors that are prospective users of a topic
- Authors that are churners of a topic

The following screenshot shows the behavior visualization page:

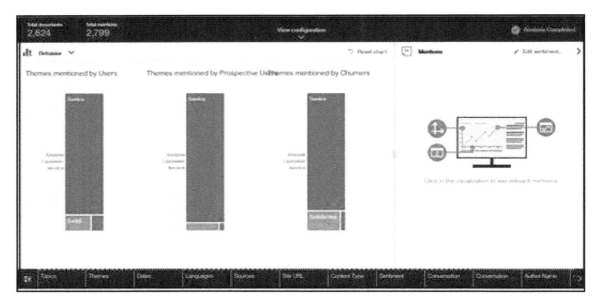

Behavior visualization page

The behavior visualization shows three individual charts. The charts are broken down by the topics that authors have exhibited this behavior against, and also by the themes mentioned by these authors. We see our project broken down by authors' use of Service, Satisfaction and Quality. Of course, as with all of the other visualizations, the behavior visualization can be filtered by right-clicking and selecting the **Exclude** button; and content is rendered in the pane at the right-hand side of the page:

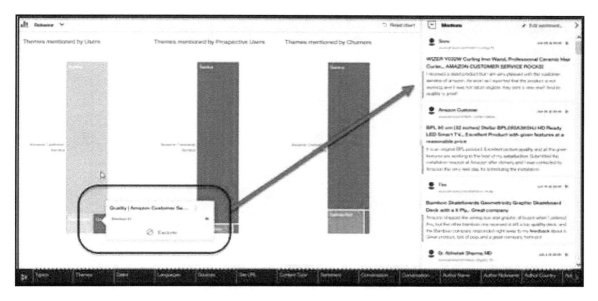

Viewing content in the right hand side pane

Demographics

In the world of social media, it is important to understand demographics. The Watson Analytics for Social Media demographics visualization analyzes your project's mentions by gender, marital status, and parental status automatically, as shown in the following screenshots:

Demographics visualization

In our project, the demographic visualization shows that most mentions are authored by males (1028), rather than females (262), but marital status and parental status do not offer any material insights. Take a look at the following screenshot:

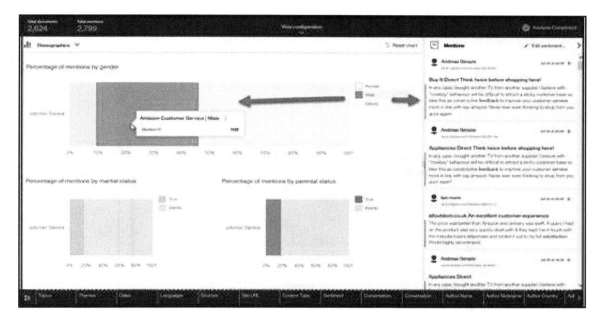

Demographic visualization offering insights

Watson Analytics determines gender by analyzing the author name, author location, and content, while marital status and parental status are determined by analyzing the author content in a mention.

The sentiment dictionary

Sentiment specifies whether a mention is positive or negative. IBM Watson Analytics for Social Media provides you with a default dictionary of sentiment terms. A sentiment term can consist of more than one word. To enhance the quality of sentiment detection, you can disable a certain positive or negative sentiment term, by making it neutral. This way, a positive or negative sentiment phrase becomes neutral term. You can also turn a specific phrase, which contains a sentiment term into a neutral. You can also add your own positive or negative terms to the sentiment dictionary. To access the sentiment dictionary, you can click on the **Edit sentiment** link in the content pane on the right-hand side of the page, as shown in the following screenshot:

Edit sentiment link in the content pane

Once you are in the sentiment dictionary, you will see all of the updated sentiment terms and have the ability to change their sentiment or add new terms of your own, as shown in the following screenshot:

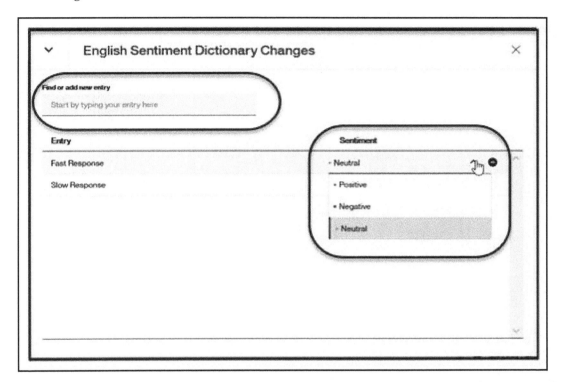

Sentimental terms are updated

The data

When you use Watson Analytics for social media and create a project, a new Social Media dataset is created for you. After the dataset is created, you can find it on the **Data** page in Watson Analytics. You'll notice the format or type of the file is listed as **Social Media Data**. Take a look at the following screenshot:

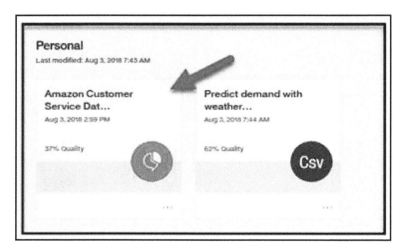

Dashboard reflecting Amazon Customer Service Dataset

Summary

In this chapter, we introduced the concept of sentiment analysis for social media projects and used Watson Analytics for Social Media to create a relevant social media project, perform an analysis, and review the results of the analysis in detail.

In the next chapter, we will tackle pattern recognition and using Watson to identify irregularities in data, in an effort to automatically classify athletes based upon provided data.

6
Pattern Recognition and Classification

In this chapter, we will be focusing on pattern recognition and using Watson Analytics to identify regularities in data, in an effort to (automatically) positionally classify athletes based upon provided data. We'll also develop a Watson Analytics project to analyze historical performance data collected on a number of professional athletes, with the objective of looking for and recognizing patterns in the data in order to predict which position on a football team the athlete may be most successful at playing.

As with our previous chapters, the breakdown for this chapter will be as follows:

- The problem defined
- Starting a pattern recognition and classification project
- Developing a pattern recognition and classification project
- Reviewing the results

The problem defined

The technical definition of pattern recognition is as follows: the calling out or identification (recognition) of patterns and regularities in data based on prior knowledge or the information extracted from the pattern.

Pattern recognition is considered by some to be a mature but still exciting and fast developing field, underpinning developments in cognitive fields such as computer vision, image processing, text, document analysis, and even neural networks.

The discipline of pattern recognition is continuing to find applications in fast-emerging areas every day.

Using data in this way is important, in that it provides insightful analytics to help align both recruitment efforts as well as coaching and team strategies aimed at the creation of successful—or winning—teams.

How will this work? Let's think about a similar problem.

We might look at a pattern recognition use case in the venue of e-commerce. E-commerce is both promising and challenging since e-commerce has been growing significantly, and yet competitive pressure is significant. Customers are mostly not loyal, arriving via search engines and online advertisements. On search engines, they are typically presented with multiple search results, including prices, which puts pressure on margins.

Typically, these organizations develop independent processes for single or directly related information, such as which products to stock, what prices to set, and what advertisement investments might be most efficient.

Recent blog posts and information online describe what might be a common sentiment on this type of process development, that various data sources and results yielded from analytical tools still require a human expert to intervene.

Returning to our use case, athletes can be evaluated on a number of data points and performance information, which may contribute to our successful position predictions, which will (hopefully) help our team's coaching staff make informed decisions and focus on the best target athletes when recruiting for a position or positions: pattern recruiting!

Actually, *shifting* our team from **spreadsheet-based** charting and graphing of athlete data to using **Watson Analytics** for analyzing the volumes of collected data that relate to each positional need is what this project is about: we will be mainly focusing on the following:

- Freeing the team's management from simplistic two-dimensional graphical analysis by providing multidimensional
- Providing high-quality and innovative designs that are easily interchangeable, so the visualizations have the utmost impact, making it easier to recruit, draft, and train athletes by position.

Data peeking

As part of each of the Watson Analytics projects thus far in this book, we have always taken a moment to review or peek at the data we will be loading into Watson and ultimately be working with (for example, in the previous chapter, we covered this in the *Gathering and reviewing of data* section).

It's an important step in any project, even if the peek is simply a conversation with the data provider about some background and what might be expected to be in the file.

Here is what we should know in this project.

Football is one sport that is rich in data. From game results, betting/bookmaking, fantasy football leagues to the NFL Combine, the sport is overflowing with data. Let's look at the combine (as a data source).

The **NFL Scouting Combine** is a week-long showcase occurring every February, where college football players perform physical and mental tests in front of National Football League coaches, general managers, and scouts. With increasing interest in the NFL Draft, the scouting combine has grown in scope and significance, allowing personnel directors to evaluate upcoming prospects in a standardized setting (Wikipedia, 2018).

In this project, we are expecting to be supplied with data on prospective players who have participated in combine workouts, with statistics that include results by player for the following activities:

- 40-yard dash
- Bench press
- Vertical jump
- Broad jump
- 3-cone drill
- Shuttle run

In addition to this data, we'll expect to see some supplemental data based upon the player's physical attributes such as height, weight, arm length, and hand size, as well as statistics from the player's college and possibly even high school careers.

The following is a portion of our data source:

	A	B	C	D	E	F	G	H	I	J	K	L	M	N	O	P	Q	R	S	T
1	year	name	firstname	lastname	position	heightfeet	heightinch	heightinch	weight	arms	hands	fortyyd	twentyyd	tenyd	twentyss	threecone	vertical	broad	bench	round
2	2015	Ameer Abc	Ameer	Abdullah	RB	5	9	69	205	0	0	4.6	0	0	3.95	6.79	42.5	130	24	
3	2015	Nelson Agl	Nelson	Agholor	WR	6	0	72	198	0	0	4.42	0	0	0	0	0	0	0	12
4	2015	Jay Ajayi	Jay	Ajayi	RB	6	0	72	221	0	0	4.57	0	0	4.1	7.1	39	121	19	
5	2015	Kwon Alex	Alexander	OLB	6	1	73	227	0	0	4.55	0	0	4.2	7.14	36	121	24		
6	2015	Mario Alfc	Mario	Alford	WR	5	8	68	180	0	0	4.43	0	0	4.07	6.64	34	121	13	
7	2015	Javorius Al	Javorius	Allen	RB	6	0	72	221	0	0	4.53	0	0	4.28	6.96	35.5	121	11	
8	2015	Adrian Am	Adrian	Amos	FS	6	0	72	218	0	0	4.56	0	0	4.03	7.09	35.5	122	0	
9	2015	Dres Ande	Dres	Anderson	WR	6	1	73	187	0	0	0	0	0	0	0	0	0	13	
10	2015	Henry And	Henry	Anderson	DE	6	6	78	294	0	0	5.03	0	0	4.19	7.2	30	111	0	
11	2015	Rory 'Bust	Rory 'Bust	Anderson	TE	6	5	77	244	0	0	0	0	0	0	0	0	0	0	
12	2015	Stephone	Stephone	Anthony	ILB	6	3	75	243	0	0	4.56	0	0	4.03	7.07	37	122	23	
13	2015	Arik Armst	Arik	Armstead	DT	6	7	79	292	0	0	5.1	0	0	4.53	7.57	34	117	24	
14	2015	Cameron /	Cameron	Artis-Payn	RB	5	10	70	212	0	0	4.53	0	0	0	7.13	36.5	118	0	

Part of our data source

We could expect that if our team is looking to recruit for the **wide receiver** (**WR**) position, we may not be interested in a prospect's body weight, but height may be important; and perhaps a prospect's recorded time in the 40-yard dash may outshine their performance in the bench press drill. Remember, these are only suspicions—based upon an individual's personal feelings—not on data. That's where Watson Analytics can help, so read on!

The preceding table seems to be a pretty sufficient peek at the data, so let us move on now and get going with the next step in the project!

Starting a pattern recognition and classification project

Again, just like in all our projects, we need to load our data into Watson Analytics, so that we can start working with it.

We know that we can easily add data that is in a **comma-separated values** (**CSV**) or **Microsoft Excel spreadsheet** (**xls** or **xlsx**) file, and our data is CSV-formatted (so we don't need to worry about any reformatting or pre-processing), and we can just use the Watson interface to load it as we've done in previous chapters (starting form the Watson Analytic **Welcome** page, click on **Add**, select **Upload data**, and so on).

Now, Watson Analytics has our data (we see the panel here) and we are ready to get going:

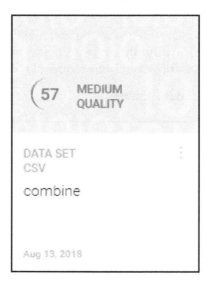

Microsoft Excel spreadsheets or CSV files can be stored anywhere that your computer or portable device has local or LAN access to. They can also be stored on a cloud storage service such as Dropbox, Box, or Microsoft OneDrive—Watson Analytics DOCs

Investigation

We've already peeked at the data and loaded it into Watson Analytics. The next step (as we've done in most of our projects so far) is to perform a more detailed review of that data using functionality provided by Watson Analytics.

In earlier projects—such as `Chapter 3`, *An Automated Supply Chain Scenario*—we initiated a formal Watson Analytics **Explore**, but just for fun let's take a slightly different approach for this project, here in this chapter:

This time, let us simply click on the panel labeled **combine** as depicted in the previous screenshot, rather than on **Add**, **Create New**, (**Explore**).

Simply clicking on the panel results in Watson Analytics providing us with some suggested starting points to help us explore our data through questioning, just like when we started by creating an **Explore**. This method is sort of a quick-start version of the Watson Analytics **Explore** and exposes the following **Here are some starting points for 'combine'** display:

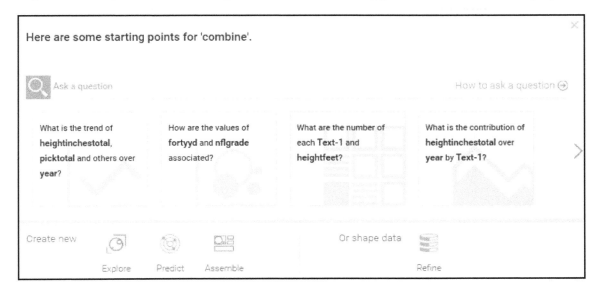

With our data file (combine), we currently have the objective of identifying patterns that can be used to assign player positions with the most accuracy. With this squarely in our minds, we can ask the question, `what affects position?`:

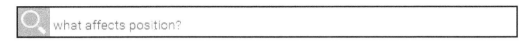

Coach me

Rather than proceeding along here to see the feedback generated from our entered question, we should point out that if you are new to Watson Analytics (or just haven't had your morning coffee yet!), there is the Watson Analytics **coach** to help you. To access the coach, you click on **How to ask a question** (shown in the upper right of the **Here are some starting points for 'combine'** display page).

When you do this, you will see various *categories* of questions; these are generated based upon the data file. You can take your time to look through the questions in each category and select actual values from drop-down lists.

1. When you have selected one of the questions, you'll see a *new set* of starting points (as shown in the screenshot here):

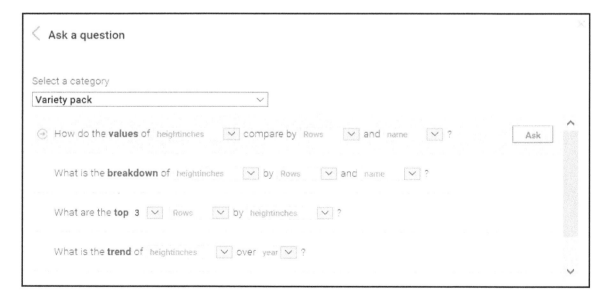

2. You'll notice that under **Select a category**, there is a drop-down list of categories and, conveniently, there is a category named **Understand relationships and identify patterns**.

3. If we make this our selection, our Watson Analytics coach shows us the following questions, intending to help us use relationships in our data to identify one or more patterns in that data:

4. Assume that we make some changes to the fields used in the first question (shown here) and then click the button labeled **Ask**:

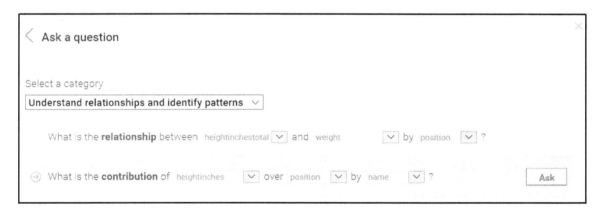

5. The response will again give us a new set of questions (as shown here):

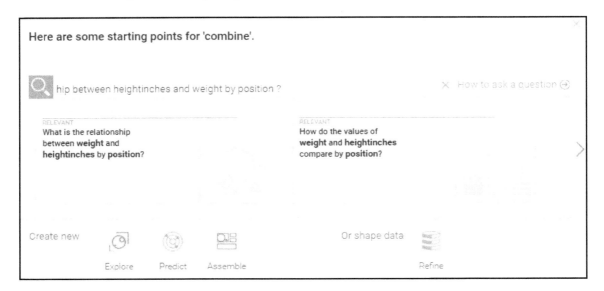

6. From here, we can drill deeper into our data using any of the provided *starting points* (or select **Create new** or **shape data**).

7. Recall that within this exploration, we can always select a starting point and then move off into other areas. For example, if we click on **What is the relationship between weight and heightinches by position?** we can see the following visualization:

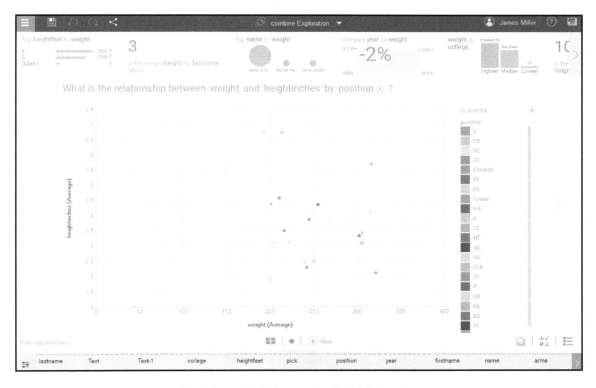

Visualization on relationship between weight and heightinches by position

8. This visualization shows the relationship of a player's weight and height to the position that they play. Wouldn't it be interesting to see the average weight and height by position? To see that, we can ask Watson, **How do the values of weight compare by position?**

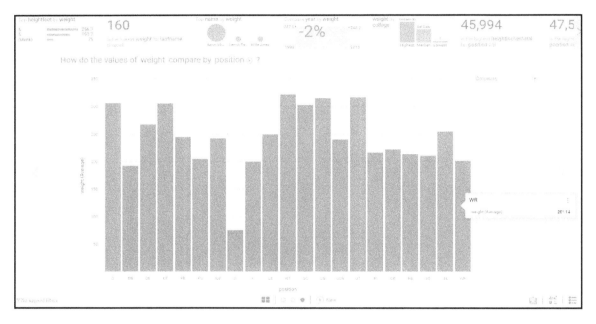

Visualization of average weight and height

9. Next, we can easily change the visualization shown by replacing **weight** with **heightfeet**, and Watson Analytics automatically applies the change:

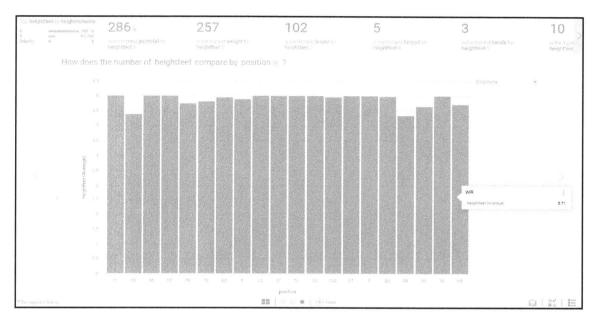

visualization shown by replacing weight with heightfeet

From this, the two insights we can see are that the average weight and height for the WR position are 5 feet 7 and just over 201 pounds (according to our data). This information begins to help us understand which player statistics may be the most relevant to the position played. You can see that, rather than constructing database query statements or filtering Excel worksheets and then reviewing tabular information, asking Watson Analytics questions and seeing the answer **visualized** is much more effective.

More with Watson Analytics

In one of the preceding visuals, we saw how height relates to position; of course, we have the ability to change any of the highlighted data fields in any visualization. Here, I changed **heightinches** (the player's height in inches) to **vertical** (the player's highest vertical jump score) and Watson Analytics dynamically updated the visualization for us:

Visualization obtained after changing heightinches to vertical jump score

From the preceding visualization, we might conclude that the heavier the athlete, the lower the vertical jump score.

The insight bar

Watson Analytics automatically identifies patterns and associations in the data and then lists new, relevant **starting points** based upon those findings for you to explore. These starting points are gathered together and displayed for you on what is known as the Watson Analytics **Insight Bar**:

position K	160	0	47.6k
has **weight** (204) for **heightfeet** 6 but only (164) for **heightfeet** 5	is the lowest average **weight** by **lastname** (Breazell)	is the lowest average **vertical** by **position** (K) and **heightfeet** (5)	is the highest total **picktotal** by **position** (WR)

View of Analytics Insight bar

The **Insight Bar** (shown previously) provides a sort of manually scrollable stock ticker, showing starting points so that they can be easily noticed, selected, and explored if desired. To view a particular starting point, you can simply click on it (see next) and then select **+New page**:

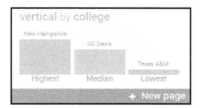

In this example, we selected the **vertical** starting point as it relates to **college,** clicked on **+New Page**, and Watson Analytics again automatically generates a new visualization for us to review, based upon that starting point, on a new page (shown in the following image):

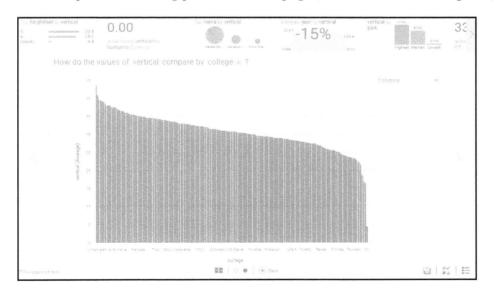

Reviewing visualization based upon that starting point

Just as with all Watson Analytics visualizations, as you refine the data that is shown in these visualizations, Watson Analytics automatically refreshes the insights bar to show the starting points that are now most relevant to the changes made within the visualization on the page.

Modifying a visualization

If we click on a data point within a visualization, we are presented with a **short menu** that allows us to either **Keep** or **Exclude** that data point from the visualization. In addition, if you click on the three-dot icon in the upper right of the menu (shown circled in the following screenshot), you can then see the extended version of that same menu:

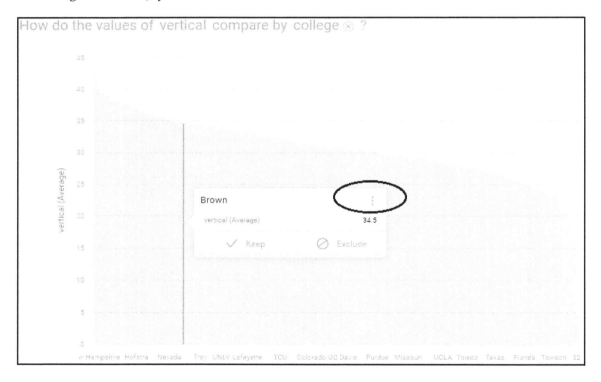

The following is a screenshot of the extended menu where you can **Keep** or **Exclude** the selected data point, but also perform some additional real-time filtering tasks:

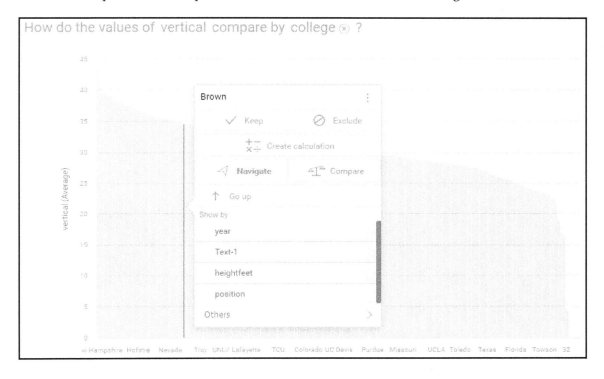

An example of this feature's usefulness is described here. During exploration, we noticed that in the following visualization a portion of the player's name (**Jr**) is erroneously showing up as a position. Rather than going back to the raw data, we can use the previously described method to select and exclude the error from our visualization:

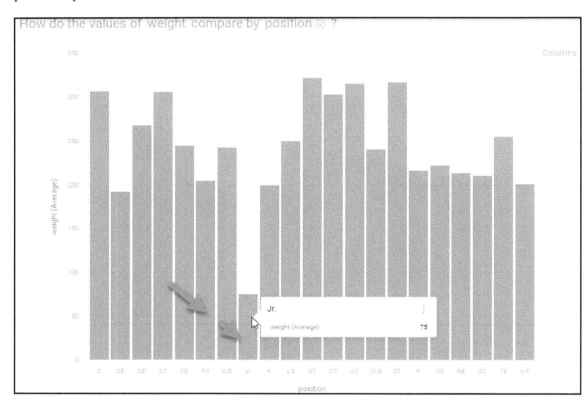

After the exclude, it looks as follows:

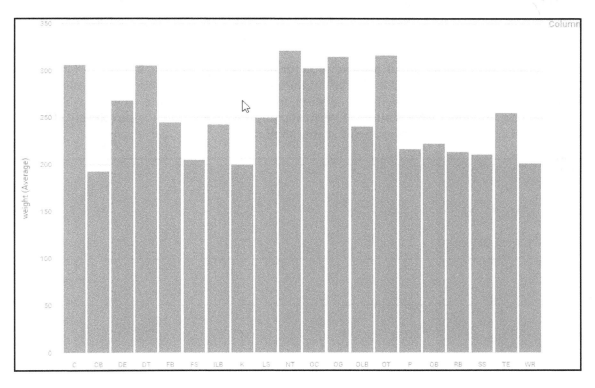

Additional filtering

We already know about **Keep** and **Exclude**. The other options available to us in the menu are as follows:

- Create calculation
- Navigate/compare
- Go up/down
- Show by

Item-based calculations

At times, you may want to create a new item that depends on the values of other items in a column of data; these are called **item-based calculations**.

For example, suppose we create a calculation for the (average) vertical jump difference between two successive years. To do this, in the following visualization, we can select an item on which we want to base the calculation. In this situation, we are viewing a visualization on **How do the values of vertical compare by year?** so we can simply click on one of the vertical bars and then click **Create calculation**:

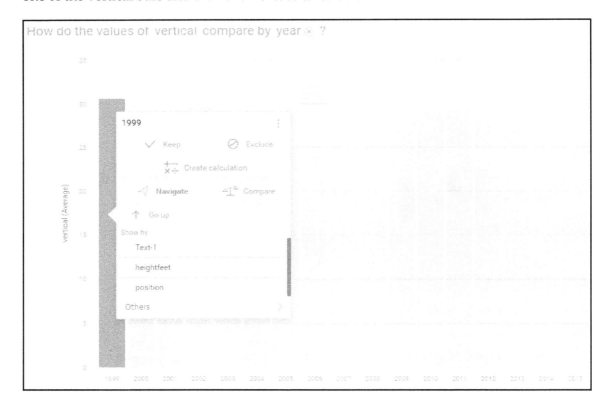

Next, in the calculation popup (shown here), we enter a name for our calculation:

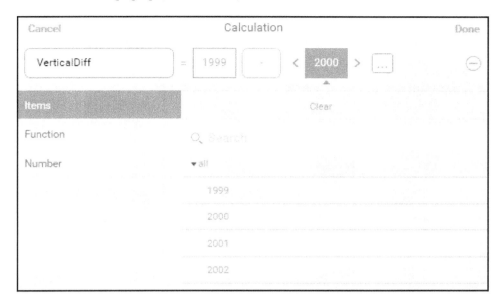

After entering the name (VerticalDiff) to be used for the calculation name, we can leave **1999** selected as the first parameter, then change the addition (+) to a subtraction (-), and finally, select **2000** as the next parameter and click **Done**.

At this point, Watson Analytics creates the calculation as a new item and it appears in the visualization! To edit the calculation, click on the new item that is based on the calculation and then click **Edit calculation**, then click **Delete**.

 These item-based calculations are only available in the exploration where you created them, and will not be stored with the data.

Navigate

Also included on the short pop-up menu, to make it easier to explore the data at different levels, gain a broader perspective, a more detailed view, or a different perspective, you can click on **Navigate** and select from a variety of options, such as **Go up**, **Go down** or a number of **Show by** selections that can affect the current visualization.

Compare

Another interesting technique to gain more insight into your data is through the use of the **Compare** feature within the same short menu we've been studying.

Clicking **Compare** gives you the ability to scroll through (using the left or right arrows) up to three different data comparison views of the selected data:

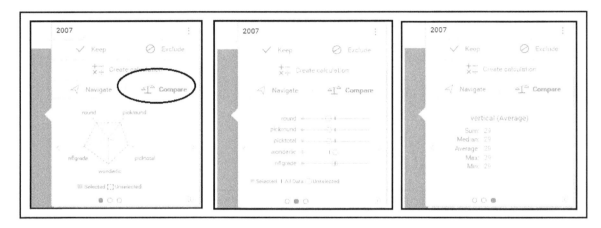

Three different data comparison views of the selected data

There are plenty of additional features to discover that allow you to explore and filter your data in various ways, starting from any individual starting point, which you will become familiar with the more you use Watson Analytics.

For now, though, let us get back to our project at hand.

Simply trending

A **trend** is the general direction of a data point over a period of time. A **pattern** is a series of data that repeats in a recognizable way. Simple examples could be the trend of average body weight first **by position**, shown in the following screenshot:

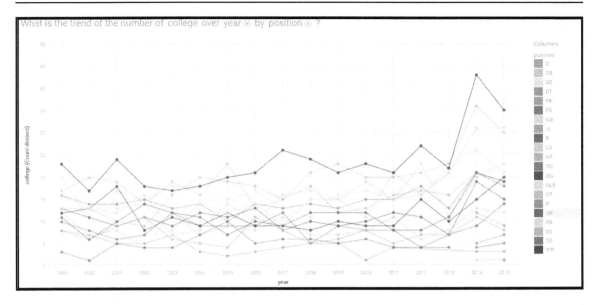

Trend of average body weight first by position

And then, the trend of average body weight for the WR position:

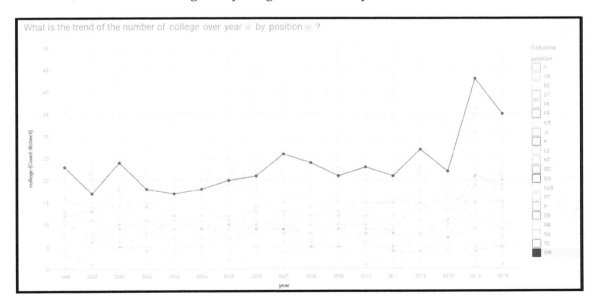

Trend of average body weight for the WR position

You can use Watson Analytics to easily create some simple trend visualizations such as the ones just shown. Again, you can just ask Watson by typing a question starting with what is the trend:

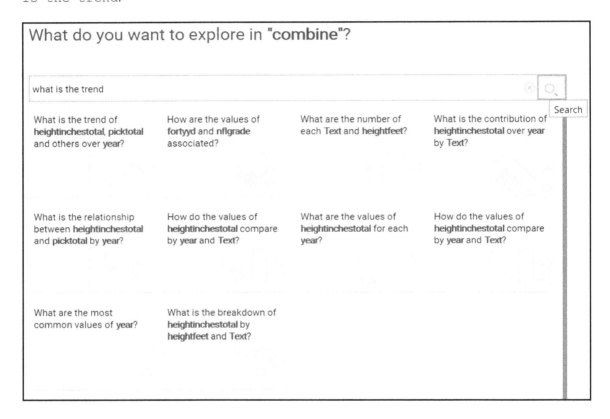

Developing the pattern recognition and classification project

The IBM Watson Analytics product documentation states that a prediction is a container for a predictive analysis and specifies the dataset that is being analyzed. A prediction can also specify the field properties that override the field properties in the dataset. By defining prediction-specific field properties, one can create custom analyses of the data.

Each Watson Analytics prediction you create can have different targets and inputs. After you create a prediction, you then review it to see the output from the analysis—and hopefully—new visual and text insights.

As a cue, the objective of this chapter's project is to determine what columns in our data affects the column position. In other words, we want to predict what combination of a player's characteristics or capabilities will best determine success for each position on a football team.

Although we have had a look at the raw data that we are using in this project, have we considered the quality of the data enough? Let's take a few moments to go back and look at our data's quality.

Quality

The fact is data quality *will* directly affect the ability to reliably predict—using IBM Watson Analytics or otherwise—any outcome. In attempt to ensure that a prediction is as good (or as strong) as it can be, Watson Analytics uses a calculated representation of its assessment of the data being used. This is known as the **data quality score**.

The data quality score is measured on a scale of 0-100 (with 100 representing the highest possible data quality). The data quality score for a data file is computed by averaging the data quality score for every field in the dataset.

When a prediction is generated by Watson Analytics, the data quality score for the data used in the prediction is displayed at the top of the **Top Predictors** page, like this:

In the preceding screenshot, we can see that our project's data is considered **Good**. Well, Good is Good, but Good is not Excellent. To see why Watson Analytics has assigned that score, you can click on the **View** link under the score text:

There are 36 issues with your data, click below to learn more this will allow you to view the **Data Quality Report**. The next section of this chapter will provide some explanation of this report in more detail.

The Watson Analytics data quality report

The IBM Watson Analytics data quality report provides both graphical and textual information about the quality of the dataset being used (as a whole as well as the individual fields in the data). You can use the data quality report to identify problematic fields within the data. The following is the data quality report generated by our combine position prediction:

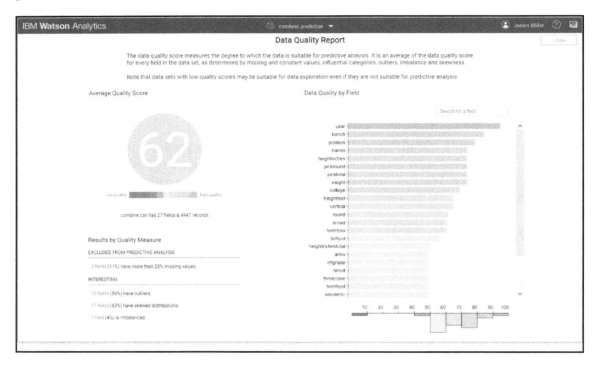

Data Quality report

If you click on any of the fields in the **Data Quality by Field** visualization, Watson Analytics will show you details about that field. For example, in line with our earlier stated assumption, we thought that a player's weight might be important in predicting which position is best for him to play. With that in mind, we can click on the **weight** field, and we see the **Mean**, **StandardDeviation**, **Min.**, **Max.**, **Distribution**, **MissingValues**, and **Outliers** for the **weight** field, as shown in the following screenshot:

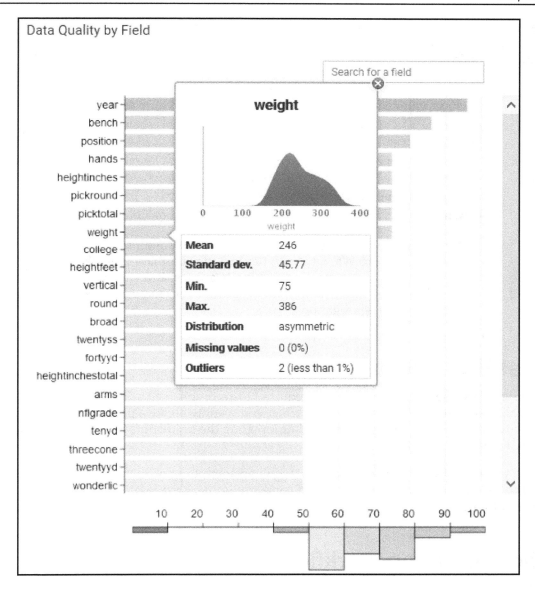

Interestingly, earlier in this chapter we saw that the average weight for WR is just over 201 pounds; here, we see the average weight overall is 246 pounds.

It is worthwhile to take just a moment to fully understand what can frequently occur within data to affect the data quality score for each individual field and the data in total. These include the following:

- **Missing values**: When a record has a field with no data in it
- **Constant values**: When some fields have the same value recorded for every field
- **Imbalance**: Occurs in a categorical field when records are not equally distributed across categories
- **Influential categories**: Those categories that are significantly different from other categories and therefore have more influence over the field
- **Outliers**: Extreme values
- **Skewness**: Measures how symmetrically a continuous field is distributed

 Simple suggestions you can use to address data quality issues before loading data into Watson Analytics include eliminating blank rows, summary rows, columns and column headings, and row headings that appear in the same cell. Also, identify and avoid the use of lookup tables, subtotals, and aggregations.

Creating the prediction

Workflows are used to define the steps required to accomplish a variety of goals. The generally accepted workflow to be used when you want to create a prediction with Watson Analytics involves adding and refining data, creating the prediction, and reviewing the generated results.

So far, we have already peeked at our data, gained something of an understanding of what it contains, loaded the data, and even did some preliminary explorations, so now we can advance to the next step: **predicting**.

The prediction workflow

The prediction workflow is as follows:

1. Add a data source.
2. Analyze the data source by creating a prediction.

3. Select up to five target fields that you want to predict. A target is a variable from your dataset that you want to understand. The target fields' outcomes are influenced by other fields (input fields) in the data. Watson Analytics automatically selects a target, but you can override this choice if another field is more important to you.

4. Watson Analytics automatically analyzes the data as the last step of the creation of your prediction.

5. When the prediction is ready, view the results. On the **Top Predictors** page, select a predictor that is interesting and open its visualization.

6. On the **Main Insight** page for the predictor that you chose, examine the top insights that were derived from the analysis.

7. Go to a **Details** page to drill into the details for the individual fields and interactions.

After you view the results, you might want to customize the prediction. You could try reducing the number of inputs to focus on the inputs that are most important. Refine the targets.

Understanding the workflow step by step

Click on **combine data set** on the **Welcome** page and click **Predict**, then skip the next step:

Complete the following steps:

1. Enter a name for this prediction in the **Name your workbook** field.
2. Review the targets. The targets are the fields of interest. They are fields that are influenced by the other fields in the dataset. The **Predict** capability defines the default targets and field properties. If a target is not a field of interest, you can click its delete icon to remove it. To add targets, you click **Select**. You must have at least one target for your prediction. You can have up to five targets. We'll select **position**.
3. Click **Create**:

Creating new analysis in Watson Analytics

4. Watson Analytics begins creating our prediction:

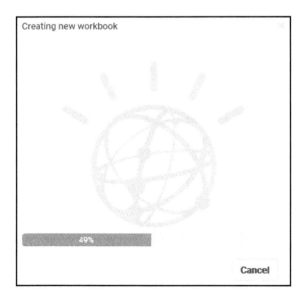

5. In a very short time, the Watson Analytics **Top Predictor** page is shown:

Watson Analytics Top Predictor

The spiral visualization on the page shows the top key drivers, or predictors, in color, with other predictors in gray. The closer the predictor is to the center, the stronger that predictor is. Out top predictors include: **weight**, **fortyyd**, and **heightinchestotal**, and the less strong predictors, **bench** and **heightinches**.

Also provided on this page are visualizations for each key predictor, giving information about what drives each behavior and outcome. If you click on one of the predictors (or hover over it), you'll see some details about it:

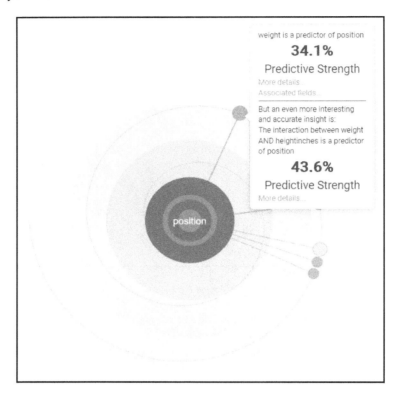

Watson Analytics states that weight is a predictor of position with a 34% **Predictive Strength**. In addition, we can also see that Watson is saying that an even more interesting and accurate insight is that the **interaction betweenweightANDheightinches** is a predictor of position and that relationship has a 43.6% **Predictive Strength**!

You'll also see some follow-up links you can access here to learn more about the predictor: **More details...** and **Associated fields....** If we click on (the first) **More details...**, we see the following insight showing the distribution of weight for each position:

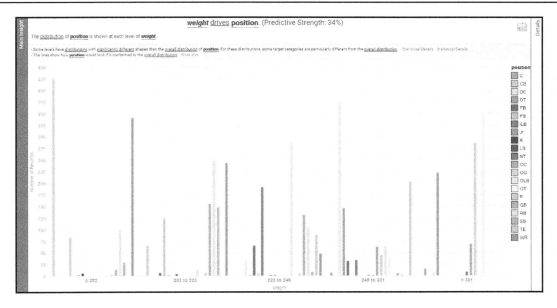

Insight showing the distribution of weight for each position

Clicking on **Associated Fields...** provides us with information on the fields that are most associated with the **weight** field:

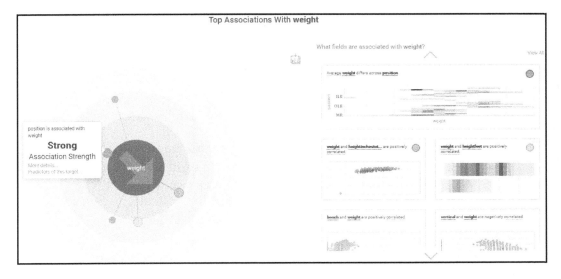

Information on the fields that are most associated with the **weight** field

And finally, the second **More details...** link drills through to information around the relationship that Watson Analytics found (**weightANDheightinches**):

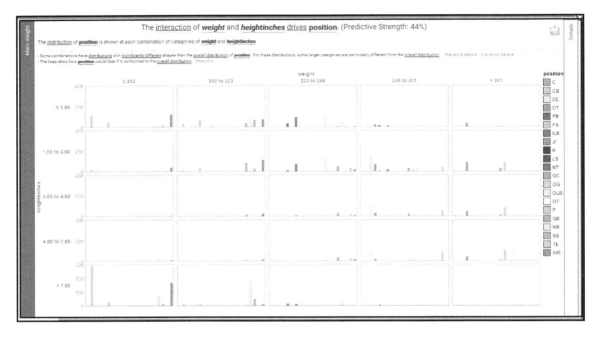

More detailed visualization

You can see that the output in predictions in Watson Analytics is a combination of both visual and textual insights, with these insights organized into insight sets, containing the following types of insights:

- **Text**: Text insights describe results. You can do the following actions with text insights:
    1. Expand text insights for supporting information.
    2. Click on a field name to view the field card. The field card displays the field's measurement level and includes a control for directly changing the field role. There is also a link to edit the field's properties.
    3. Click on a statistical term for a detailed definition.
- **Visual**: Visual insights are visualizations that support and visually demonstrate the text insights. You can move your mouse cursor over an item to view tips. In some cases, more detailed tips are available when you expand a specific text insight. Expanding some text insights can also change the visualization.

- **Dynamic**: Dynamic visual insights are dynamic changes to the visualization that result from expanding a text insight. These insights might change the visualization or use animation and highlighting to reinforce the text insight. To view the dynamic visual insight, you can click on **Show this**.

Reviewing the results

We have come to the section of the chapter—and the phase of the project—when we finish reviewing the output generated by Watson Analytics, hopefully identify several insights, and try to draw a reasonable conclusion.

We started with a pretty clear assumption: if our team is looking to recruit for the **wide receiver (WR)** position, we may not be interested in a prospect's body weight, but height may be important; and perhaps a prospect's recorded time in the 40-yard dash may outshine their performance in the bench press drill. We've already done some exploring and reviewing at this point, so let's see if the data agrees with that assumption.

During our explorations, we gathered insights such as height and weight by position, as well as specific averages for these physical statistics for players playing WR. We also generated some trend visualizations. Here in this final section, we will try to draw some conclusions based upon the output generated by Watson Analytics, and see how those conclusions stack up to our original assumptions.

Displaying top predictors and predictive strength

Pattern recognition is the process of taking in raw data, and applying actions on it, such as classifying the input data into classes based on key features. With this in mind, in this chapter's exercise, we want to be able to organize various key fields within the combine data into positional (position) groups. In other words, group player height, weight (and/or other physical characteristics of the athlete), as well as combine drill scores into position groups. Perhaps we can find the characteristics for a **WR** group?

Once we have our prediction displayed in Watson Analytics, go through following steps:

1. We can click on the **View All** option (near the upper right of the page shown next) to display the charts with the ranking of the top predictors and their respective predictive strength value:

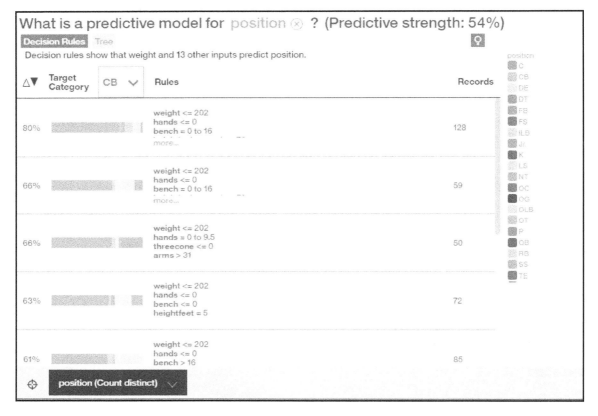

Display charts with ranking of the top predictors and their respective predictive strength value

2. Each predictive strength value is displayed in parentheses after each predictor. The strongest predictor is on top. We see that Watson Analytics has found the weight is the top predictor for position, followed by **fortyyd, heightinchestotal**, and **bench**:

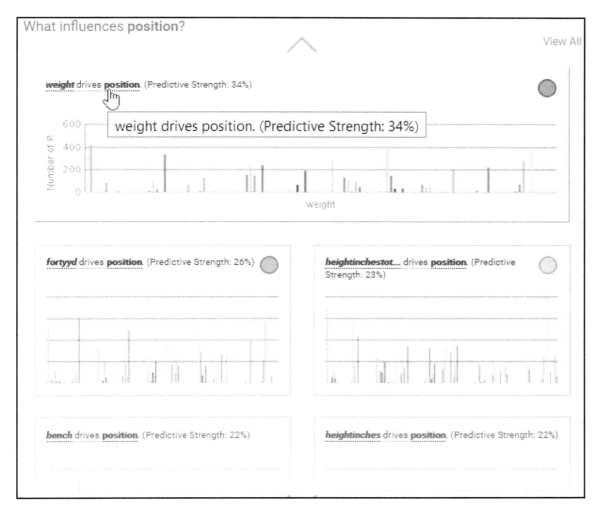

Visualization displaying weight is the top predictor for position, followed by fortyyd, heightinchestotal, and bench

3. To see the statistical details behind each predictor, you can click on a **predictor chart**. From the **Main Insight** page, you can then select to show or hide specific statistical details:

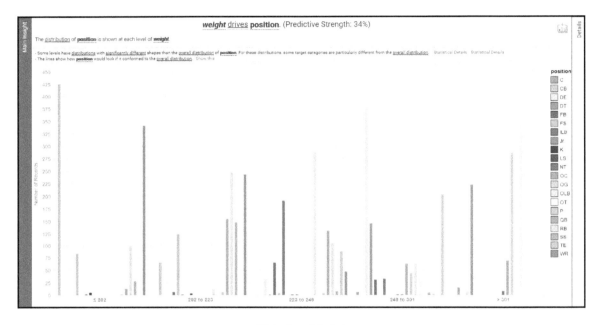

Viewing the predictor chart

So, let's summarize. Focusing on the strongest positional predictors for the WR position, the perfect player prospect has an average weight of 201 pounds and just over 6 foot tall. Their performance in the 40-yard dash is 4.5, and the bench drill is 6.37.

Here are the results of our project, summarized using the Watson Analytics **Assemble** functionality:

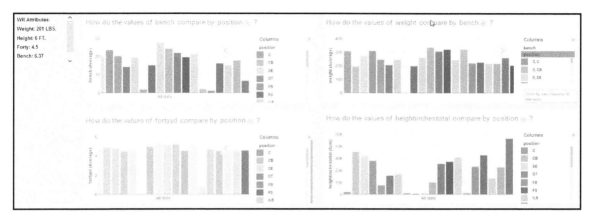

Results of our projects

In conclusion, we can see that what we assumed (height, weight, and speed being the most important attributes of a potential WR) is indeed of the most interest for a WR; this seems to match what Watson Analytics is telling us (at least based upon the given data)!

Summary

In this chapter, we focused on pattern recognition and using Watson Analytics to identify regularities in data, in an effort to (automatically) positionally classify athletes based upon the provided data. We made some preliminary assumptions, based upon a peek at the player statistics data provided, loaded it into Watson Analytics, created a prediction, and ultimately aligned the outcomes with our original assumptions.

In the next chapter, we will introduce the concept of personalized recommendations and the use of Watson to create a specialized plan through conversations. In that chapter, the objective will be to create an individualized plan based upon characteristics found within a pool of data.

7
Retail and Personalized Recommendations

In this chapter, we will be concentrating on the concept of personalized recommendations and the use of Watson Analytics to create specialized plans through conversational behaviors found within data.

In this chapter's project, our objective will be to create an individualized plan based on a type of user's prior activities and characteristics found within a designated pool of data.

As with our previous chapters, the breakdown for this chapter will be as follows:

- The problem defined
- Starting the project
- Developing the project
- Reviewing the results

The problem defined

A personalized recommendation is pretty simple in concept. In its most basic form, it just means to present or offer someone only those options for a particular situation that have the highest probability of being chosen by that individual, or in a kind of hands-on sense, presenting merchandise or promotional items that will have the highest probability of being purchased by that type of individual.

These recommendations are characteristically made based on *experienced user behavior* such as user purchases, page views, clicks, and even items a user has added to a (shopping) cart but perhaps hasn't actually purchased.

These recommendations are not made simply because they visually coordinate, come from the same collection, or are made by the same manufacturer, and so on.

If you do the research, the most common theme around personalized recommendations is that:

> *A personalized product recommendation isn't based on an assumption or guess. Personalized recommendations are based on specific user behavior(s).*

Product recommendation engines

These days, it is quite common to come across **product recommendation engines,** which utilize Artificial Intelligence (machine learning) to enhance the shopping experiences for customers of online stores. This technique has become extremely prevalent and effective within the fashion industry where visuals may direct the buying decision of a customer (for example, accessories and such are matched with whatever the customer has purchased or has shown an interest in).

A product recommendation engine, also sometimes known as an **e-commerce personalization engine**, is designed to give product cues to the user that are *visually related* to current product choices. This helps a customer pick the right fashion apparel with a somewhat different cut, model, color, pattern, or size from their original choice.

A recommendation system can be used to serve customers with personalized online product recommendations, resulting in more *upselling* and *cross-selling,* consequently improving conversion rates and reducing cart abandonment.

Recommendation systems are setting a new standard within the industry for customer engagement and brand recognition.

Recommendations from Watson Analytics

Although we won't be using Watson Analytics as an online recommendation engine, it does make practical sense for us to use Watson Analytics as the tool to analyze user behavior data and then provide recommendations based upon Watson's ability to identify **predictors** with the highest prediction strength.

Predictive strength measures how well a predictor variable accurately predicts a target. You use predictive strength to compare the various predictors within your data. Predictive strength is typically presented as a percentage. A predictor with a predictive strength of 100% perfectly predicts a target. A predictor can be a single input or a combination of inputs. We'll see this work later in this chapter.

 The fundamental statistical test that determines predictive strength depends on the measurement level of the target. For categorical targets, predictive strength is the proportion of correct classifications. For continuous targets, predictive strength is 1—relative error.

As an example of user recommendation, everyone should know about the www.amazon.com website, and most are likely to also be aware that when Amazon recommends a product on its site, it is not a making a random, or chance, recommendation.

In an article found in *Fortune*, the following explains:

> *At root, the retail giant's recommendation system is based on a number of simple elements: what a user has bought in the past, which items they have in their virtual shopping cart, items they've rated and liked, and what other customers have viewed and purchased. Amazon calls this homegrown math item-to-item collaborative filtering, and it's used this algorithm to heavily customize the browsing experience for returning customers. A gadget enthusiast may find Amazon web pages heavy on device suggestions, while a new mother could see those same pages offering up baby products (Amazon's recommendation secret; Mangalindan, 2012).*

In this chapter, we will use a file of logged online user behaviors in an effort to identify opportunities for an upstart online retail store to kick-start a program aiming to provide unique individual online shopping experiences.

The premise of this new store is to use Watson Analytics to evaluate available user behavior data, looking at data (either volunteered by the user or determined automatically by the website) to create a customized user experience for each user each time they visit the store's website, in an effort to increase sales.

Information such as images and/or advertisements that were clicked on, previously completed and abandoned purchases, as well as user demographical statistics, will hopefully be used as sources to guide the creation of focused marketing campaigns, coupon offers, and even the look and feel and navigation style of the website, for each shopper.

The data at a glance

At this point in the book, with any luck, we have established a familiar project cadence. That is, after a brief dialogue on the objectives of our project, the next step has always been to have a high-level peek at the actual raw data we will be using in the project.

Let's say that in this project we have been provided the following information about the available data:

- The data gathered for us is based on user online user sessions over periods of time and is in the form of a formatted MS Excel report
- We expect that the data includes various data points about the session, such as time online, date/timestamps, ads and links clicked on, products browsed, products added to cart, products purchased, where the session was initiated, and so on
- Various demographical information has been added to the data, which includes specific details on the user as well as the products involved in the user sessions, including those product's historic performance

As we have been demonstrating, it is quite easy to load data into Watson Analytics, but before loading the data into IBM Watson Analytics, its advantageous for us to perform some data preparation to ensure that all of the analyses we'll perform are as accurate as possible. Since our data is being provided to us as an MS Excel formatted worksheet, let's take a look at it.

Opening the file in Excel, we see a pretty report:

Scrolling through the data, we notice several things:

- There is Excel conditional formatting applied
- There are descriptive/useful column headings
- Some subtotal lines (this one shows `Dollar Amount Sold` by `Product ID Purchased`) and other total lines are present:

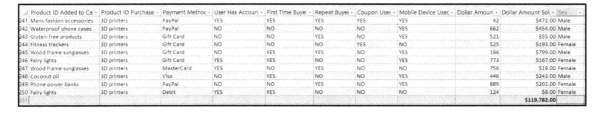

Dollar Amount Sold by Product ID Purchased columns

Generally speaking, conditional formatting aimed at coloring and arranging for readability doesn't help or hurt Watson Analytics, but as a rule, you should strip it out of the file before loading it.

Some of the *must do* data preparation tasks include the following:

- Remove filters and hidden rows or columns
- Remove total lines/columns as well as nested lines and columns
- Verify that all columns have names

Since our data is Excel-based, it's an easy (although manual) process to perform the data reformatting. Once we've accomplished the cleanup, we can save our data as an unformatted CSV file, a portion of which is shown as follows in Windows Notepad:

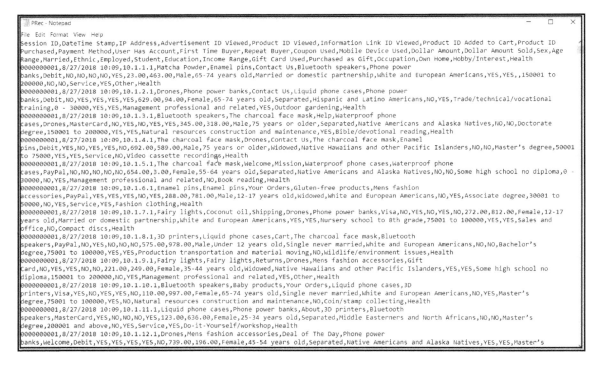

Data file

Now the data can be loaded into Watson Analytics without concern:

Starting the project

Let's get going.

In Watson Analytics **Refine**, it is easy to test our data quality column by column (click **Refine**, select our file, then click on the Data Metrics icon, which is shown as follows):

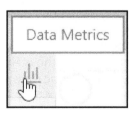

It would seem that there are plenty of columns that have very high (98 or above) data quality scores, for example, **Advertisement ID**, **Age Range**, **Ethnic,** and so on. This not only gives us confidence in whatever predictions Watson may come up with, but also affords us the ability to further refine our data to focus more on the specific needs or interests we may have.

For example, suppose we want to establish personal recommendations based upon user behavior of a certain *age range*? Or perhaps *user ethnicities*?

Initially, we are going to target those users who fall into the following categories:

- Retirees (65 -74 years old and older than 75 years too)
- Caucasian (White and European Americans)
- Making a purchase for the first time (First Time Buyer)

To narrow down our file to contain only activity for this user group, we can use Watson Analytics **Refine** filters. The following describes the steps to create filters on our dataset:

1. In **Refine**, we start by clicking the Actions icon:

2. Next, we can click on the appropriate column heading in the dataset.

 If the column contains only numeric values, you can use the provided sliders to specify a range of the values that you want; alternatively, you can enter those values directly. If the column contains only text or date values, you can click on the specific date values to include.

3. In the following screenshot, I have added a filter on the data column named **Age Range** and included only those age groups that would indicate that the user is most likely retired:

4. Once you have added a filter to a data column, Watson Analytics adds a *blue line* or *blue dashes* to the column name to indicate that the data in that column is filtered. A brief description of the filter also appears on the column name. In the following screenshot, you can see the blue dashes, as well as the text **3 of 9,** which indicates that I have chosen only 3 of the 9 available values for this data column:

5. We will continue filtering our dataset by adding filters to the **Ethnic** data column, shown as follows:

6. We will also do this for the **First Time Buyer** data column:

Range filter

There is one last refinement we want to make to our dataset. We are particularly interested in those users whose purchase total was within a particular range, perhaps between $75 and $125 USD. Again, this is simply accomplished with the Watson Analytics **Refine/Filter** feature.

To add a range filter, you can click on the **Dollar Amount Sold** data column and use the sliders or, if it is easier, you can click on the range values themselves and directly enter your amounts (75 and 125):

Whoa there! Once we apply that filter, our dataset is reduced to only three records:

Evidently, the idea of focusing on a dollar purchased amount range (remember that this data already has been filtered) is not a valid (or useful) assumption for our project!

With this in mind, we'll go back and adjust the range to between $1 and $999 so that we can ensure that we will have a good number of data records to work with.

Save me

Once we have completed making our refinements to our dataset, we need to save the refined dataset to a **New** file. To do this, you can click the Save icon and enter a name for the new file (you will observe that the default file name will have the word **Refinement** appended to the end of the original dataset name). You will also need to select the location to save the file (the default, **Personal area,** is fine):

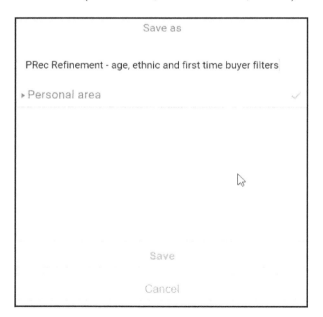

Note that our original dataset is not changed in any way. The refined dataset is saved, and it appears on the Watson Analytics **Welcome** page as a refined dataset, which differentiates it from a regular dataset. From there, we can click on the dataset to create a prediction, exploration, or view based on it:

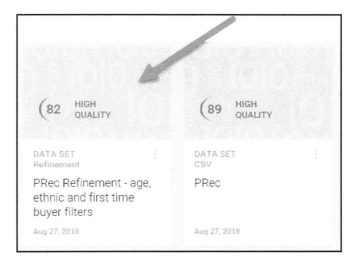

We are now ready to move along with our project, using our refined (or **Refinement**) dataset.

Developing the project

To continue with project development, we can again utilize the Watson Analytics **Explore** feature. If you don't quite remember how to do this, from the **Welcome** page you can click on **Explore** and then select the dataset to be explored, which in our case is the data we just finished filtering (using **Refine**) in the previous section.

Watson Analytics will present you with various *starting points*:

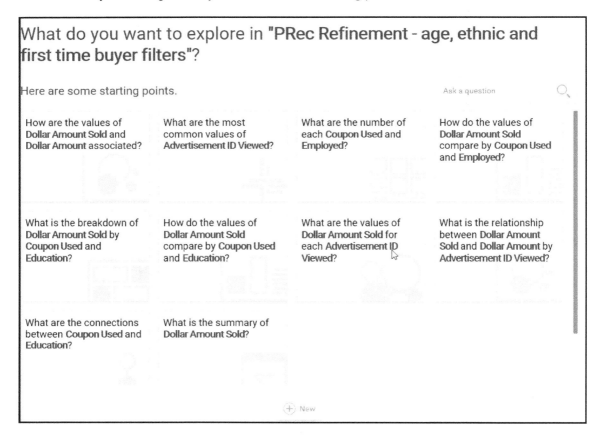

IBM Watson Analytics uses questions rather than SQL commands to generate the list of starting points that you can use to create visualizations that meet your needs.

Not surprisingly, we are interested most in the `Dollar Amount Sold`, and particularly the relationship between `Dollar Amount` and `Dollar Amount Sold`.

These *data points* in our file constitute the average amount (in dollars) that a user has in their online shopping cart, compared to the average amount they actually spend.

The following is an interesting Watson Analytics visualization showing how various advertisements a user views on the website may (or may not) affect this relationship:

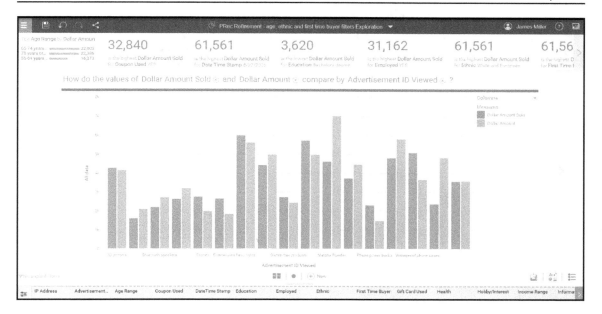

Searching for other predictors, we might alter the previous visualization to look at the effects of the user's education:

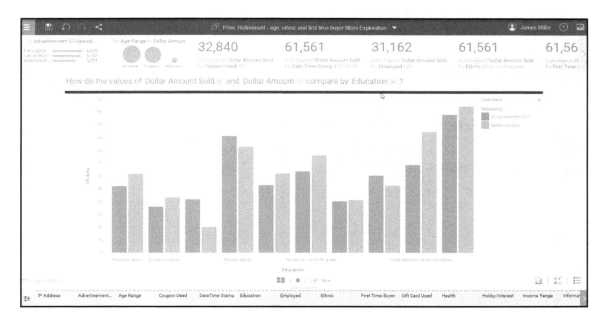

Or, We could look at age (range):

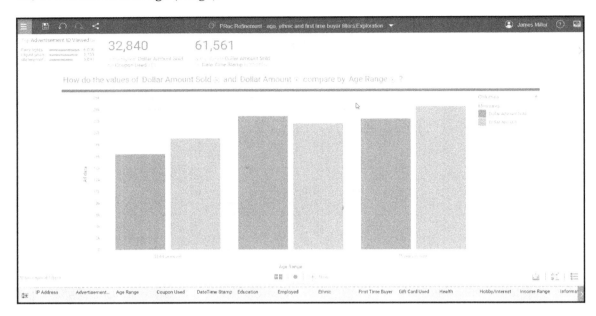

Of course, as an alternative to reviewing insights that Watson created for us, you can always start a related exploration by clicking on **+New** at the bottom of an insight or visualization page. When you click **+New**, Watson Analytics directs you back to the **Starting Point** page where you can again select one of the starting points provided, or enter your own new keywords and then click on one of the new starting points that will appear.

Using this approach, we can have Watson Analytics create a rich visualization to answer this query: how might the *amount sold* break down by *education* and whether the user was using a *mobile device*.

The following is Watson's answer expressed in a rich, easily understood visualization:

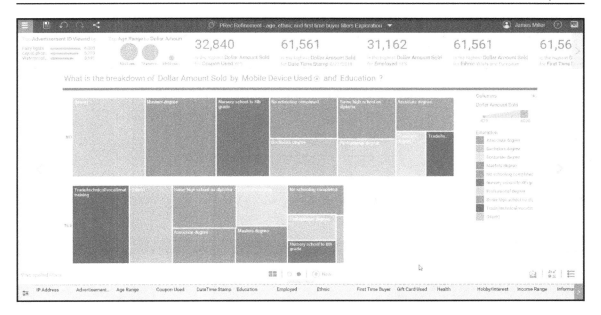

Married Status and **Education** also produce thought-provoking visualizations:

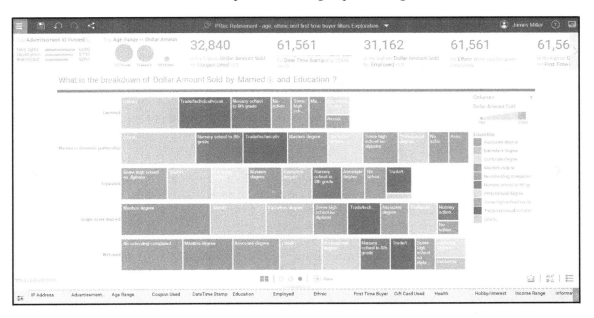

After we have done some proper exploration on our data, we may find that we have many pages of different visualizations created. At the bottom of each page, you will see that the current page is indicated by a *solid circle icon*. To move to another page, you can click a different circle. There is one circle for each page:

You can also view all pages at the same time, making it easier to select the one page or visualization that you want. To see all of the pages in a tiled format (shown as follows), you can click on the tile icon:

The yield from performing a **Watson Analytics Exploration** on a dataset should be the identification of the data points within the data that are of interest to your project's objectives. After an **Exploration**, you should have a reasonable idea of what to create a prediction on (what to predict) and, possibly, what the best or strongest predictors might be.

During an exploration, you should create many visualizations using a natural language, rather than program code or SQL commands, to enter questions that find various starting points for exploring your data. You also can use keywords along with column headings and data values found in your dataset to build your questions.

For example, in one of our previous questions, *what is the breakdown of dollar amount and dollar amount sold by age range?*, breakdown is a **keyword**, age is a **column heading**, and Dollar Amount Sold is a **data value**.

IBM Watson Analytics makes it very easy to quickly create and compare multiple visualizations during an exploration by using bar charts, bubble charts, tree maps, and other visualization types, which you can then reuse and share later. You can set aside these visualizations to use in dashboards and infographics using Watson Assemble. You can also share those visualizations with others by emailing the visualizations as an image, presentation, and Adobe PDF files. We'll try sharing our insights in the next section of this chapter.

Reviewing the results

Now that we have done the work, although Watson Analytics does a lot of the work for us, we are in a good place in that we are ready to create a **prediction**.

Remember that our goal was to determine what kind of personal recommendation could be made to promote more purchases by our focus group of Caucasian retirees who were first-time buyers.

As a short review, to create our Watson Analytics prediction, you can do the following :

1. Go to the Watson Analytics Welcome page and then click on **Predict**
2. Of course, we need data, so we must then select our dataset from the list in the **Create new prediction** box
3. Enter a name for our new prediction in the **Name your workbook** field:

Targets

It is very important to review your project's prediction **targets**. The targets are the fields of interest in the prediction. They are fields that are influenced by the other fields in the dataset. The Watson Analytics Predict capability defines default targets and field properties for you. Watson Analytics attempts to provide us with what it *thinks* are the fields we are interested in. Here, Watson lists `Purchased as Gift`, `Product ID Purchased`, and `Dollar Amount Sold` as default fields we may be interested in, based upon our dataset. These are all very good *guesses*, but in this project, we only care about `Dollar Amount Sold`, so we can click on the Delete icon to remove the other two fields:

If we wanted to add more targets, we could click on **Select target**. Note that you must have at least *one* target for any prediction and you are limited to up to five targets.

When we have finished reviewing and editing our targets and predictors, we click on the button labeled **Create**. A message shows the progress Watson is making as the prediction is created. When the prediction process completes, you can view the summary for the prediction and explore the output in detail.

The following is the **Summary** page of our Watson Analytics prediction:

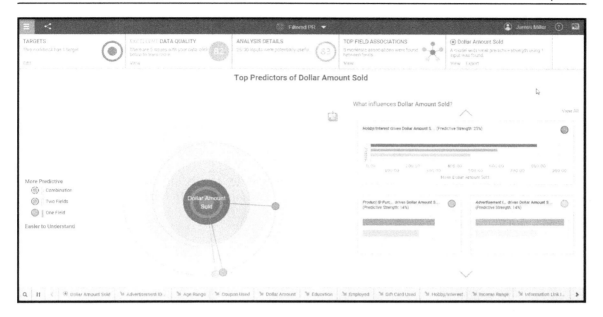

Summary ribbon

Across the top of the **Top Predictors** page is what I refer to as the *summary ribbon* of the predictive model generated by Watson Analytics. The summary ribbon includes thumbnail images showing the following information:

- **Targets**
- **Data Quality (score)**
- **Analysis Details**
- **Top Field Associations**
- **Model Highlight**

An explanation of what information each thumbnail provides is given here:

- **Targets thumbnail**:

The targets thumbnail lists the targets defined in the model. In our example, we have one target, `Dollar Amount Sold`. You also can click **Edit** and change the targets in the model.

- **Data Quality thumbnail**:

The **data quality score** measures the degree to which the data used in the model is appropriate to be utilized for **predictive analysis**. It is an average of the data quality score for every field in the dataset, as determined by missing and constant values, influential categories, outliers, imbalance, and skewness. If you click on **View**, you will see the column by column breakdown of data quality scores. In our project, the fields we are interested in, `Dollar Amount Sold`, `Age Range`, `Ethnic`, and `First Time Buyer` ,all have high data quality scores, or we have filtered on them, so we will move on to the next statistic.

- **Analysis Details thumbnail**:

The Analysis Details thumbnail tells you the total number of columns in your dataset that were considered in the predictive analysis(referred to as inputs), as well as the number of those inputs that could potentially affect the target. In other words, of the 30 columns of data in the file, Watson Analytics considered using 25 of them as predictors.

- **Top Field Associations thumbnail**:

In statistics, the **association of fields** is any statistical relationship, whether causal or not, between two random variables, data. Watson Analytics reviews each and every column of data in the model to determine where relationships exist. The top field associations thumbnail gives us the result of that analysis. If you click on the **View** link in this thumbnail, you can see the relationships:

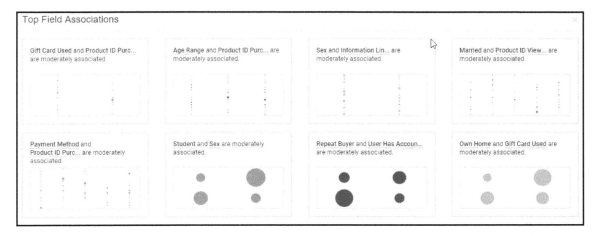

- **Model Highlight thumbnail**:

In the Model Highlight thumbnail, Watson Analytics indicates what the predictive target is (`Dollar Amount Sold`) and provides a brief summary of the model results.

Our initial model is considered to have *weak predictive strength* using one input predictor (Hobby/Interest). As of this writing, the **Export** link isn't enabled, but **View** will show the detailed results of this summary:

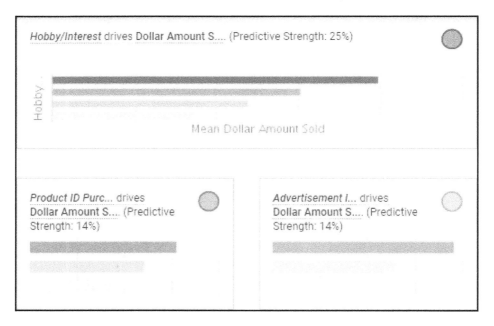

The top predictors

Having now created several predictions (or predictive models) throughout the other chapters of this book, you no doubt have noticed that when you create a new prediction in Watson Analytics, the prediction opens automatically so you can view it. While you are viewing a prediction, you can see a summary of the most important insights in your data (that is, the **Summary** or **Top Predictors** page) and explore specific fields in detail (by just clicking on them).

Again, the spiral visualization—referred to by some as the *predictive bullseye*—on the **Top Predictors** page shows the top key drivers, or predictors, in color, with other found predictors in gray. The closer the predictor is to the center of the spiral or *bullseye*, the stronger that predictor is.

There is also a visualization for each key predictor, giving you information about what drives each behavior and outcome. If you click on one of the predictors (or hover over it), you see some details about it:

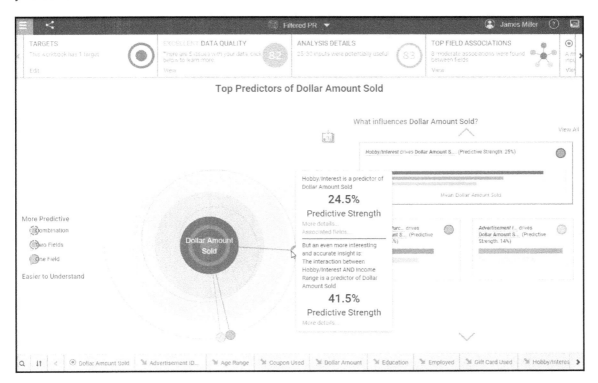

In our project's prediction, Watson Analytics has found that the **Hobby/Interest** column of data, is the top predictor of **Dollar Amount Sold,** but has a weak predictive strength (24.5%). More interesting though (as Watson directly points out) is that if we couple **Hobby/Interest** with **Income Range**, the two together have a much stronger predictive strength (41.5%).

The details of this relationship are visible if we click on the **More details...** link, and are shown here over two pages, the **Main Insight** page and the **Details** page:

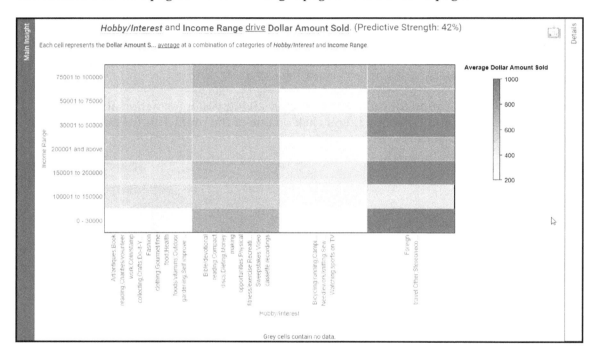

The following screenshot shows you the **Details** page:

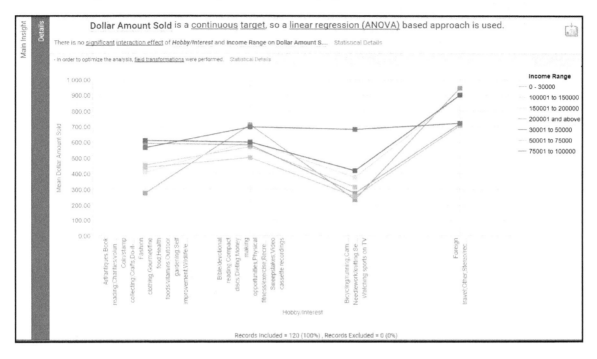

As with most features of Watson Analytics, rich visualizations along with detailed text explanations are generated and used to communicate key points and insights found in the data. For example, on the preceding **Details** page, we see this:

Dollar Amount Sold is a continuous target, so a linear regression (ANOVA) based approach is used.

Most of the textual insights and/or explanations contain hyperlinks so if you want to learn more about a term (such as **linear regression**), you can click on it:

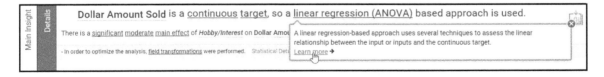

Once again, the predict strength of the combination of **Hobby/Interest** with **Income Range** is just 41.5%. With a little effort, we can use Watson Analytics to improve on that percentage. That is, if we go back to the **Top Predictors** page and select **Combination** (under **More Predictive**), we can see that **Education** and **Income Range** together produce a predictive strength of 53.2 % (shown here):

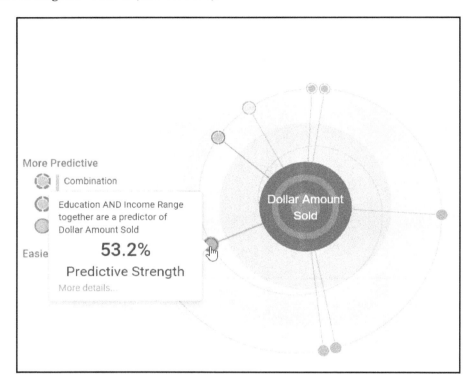

Sharing the insights

We mentioned sharing insights earlier in this chapter and the preceding insight is worth sharing, so let's see how we can do that with the Watson Analytics Assemble feature. You use the Assemble capability to convey/share the analysis and insights that were discovered in Predict (and also Explore). To make sharing efficient, when you come across something you may want to share later, do the following:

1. You should add it to your collection by clicking the **Collect** icon, shown as follows:

2. Once a visualization has been added to the collection, you can (from the **Welcome** page) click on **Assemble**:

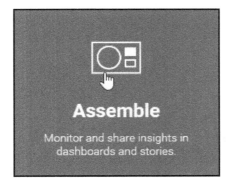

3. From there, you will see the **Create new view** dialog (shown next) where you can click on **Skip** (since we know we are going to share from our collection):

4. After clicking **Skip**, you can choose a template style to build. I clicked to select a **Tabbed** dashboard and a single, non-freeform tabbed layout, then clicked **Create**:

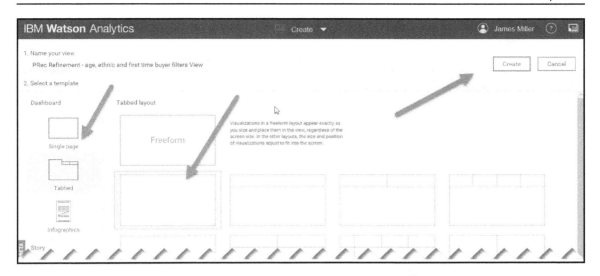

5. Now we are in edit mode, so we can click on the Collection icon to see our collection of assets and select the visualization we want to share:

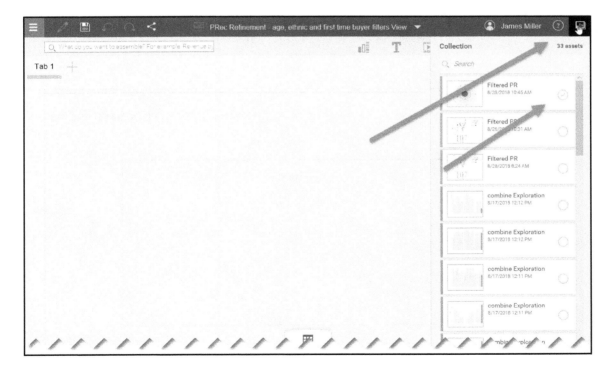

6. Now that we see our collected Assets, we can drag and drop them onto the template:

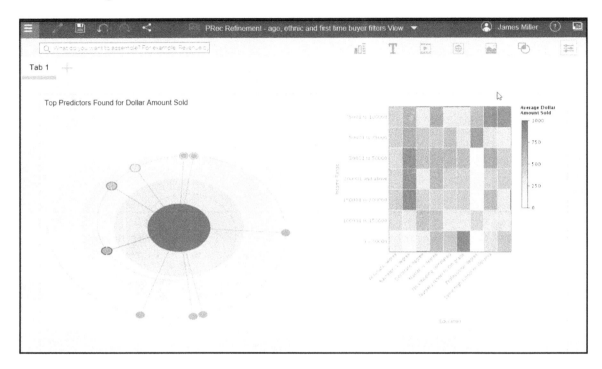

7. Once you have assembled what you want to share, you can click **Save** and name your creation:

8. Once it is saved, you can click the Share icon in the toolbar area:

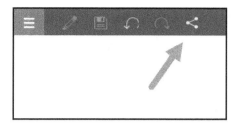

9. And from the **Share** dialog, you can select how or in what format you want to share your insight:

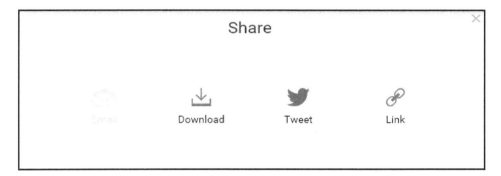

10. As an example, I selected **Download**:

Summary

In this chapter, a Watson Analytics project was used to create an individualized plan based upon characteristics found within a pool of user behavior data. The plan focused on Caucasian retirees who were first-time buyers. What Watson found was that for this type of user, **Education** and **Income Range** together are strong predictors of whether a user will make a purchase.

In the next chapter, we will discuss integrating IBM Watson Analytics with an organization's forecasting system to test an organization's product sales forecasting effectiveness, comparing forecasts to actual results.

8
Integration for Sales Forecasting

In this chapter, we will be discussing the concept of integrating Watson Analytics with an organization's forecasting system in order to improve the organization's product sales forecasting effectiveness. We will do this by gaining more in-depth knowledge of available data as well as (hopefully) identifying new insights to product performances.

The breakdown for this chapter will be the usual format:

- The problem defined
- Starting the project
- Developing the project
- Reviewing the results

The problem defined

Forecasting is the process of *making predictions* for the future based on past and present data and, perhaps some trend analysis. A common example might be estimating sales for a particular product line.

Product forecasting

Product forecasting is the **science of predicting the degree of success a new product will enjoy in the marketplace**. To do this, the forecasting model must take into account such things as product awareness, distribution, price, fulfilling unmet needs, and competitive alternatives.

Typical forecasting techniques include the following:

- **Delphi**: A group of field experts respond to a series of questionnaires
- **Scenario**: The forecaster generates different outcomes based on different starting criteria or scenarios
- **Subjective**: This allows forecasters to predict outcomes based on their subjective thoughts and feelings
- **Time series**: This measures data gathered over time to identify trends

Systematic forecasting

In the past, forecast analysts relied heavily on tools such as MS Excel to do forecasting, planning, and reporting. Although Excel is a mature tool that most (all?) finance folk know well, it can become overly labor-intensive when dealing with large amounts of data and is usually difficult to maintain for versioning of a forecast.

At some point, most organizations have addressed this by installing and maintaining some sort of software system that specializes in the ability to store data, maintain versions, and also allow for slicing and dicing data into professional styled reports.

The advent of such a tool which provides these features as well as others will, most definitely, drive financial management efficiency, deliver stronger business foresight, and steer business performance effectively.

IBM Planning Analytics

There are plenty of tools in the market that support some, if not all, of an organization's forecasting and reporting needs; however this book is not about forecasting tools, so there is no advantage in detailing and debating which tool to use—we'll just pick one of the better ones, that is, IBM Planning Analytics.

If you are not familiar with the tool, the following may provide a bit of perspective:

"IBM Planning Analytics is a planning, budgeting, forecasting, and analysis solution, available for deployment on-premise or in the cloud. Built on the technology of IBM Cognos TM1, it helps organizations automate manual, spreadsheet-based processes and link financial plans to operational tactics. IBM Planning Analytics features a customizable workspace that can be deployed to cost center owners and business managers. It also offers a Microsoft Excel interface."

- (IBM.com)

Another fine reason for choosing this tool is that IBM Planning Analytics not only empowers users, but facilitates practices such as *driver-based planning* and *rolling forecasts*. Users of IBM Planning Analytics can perform complex dimensional calculations to analyze product profitability, sales mix, and price/volume variance, and so on.

Perhaps the most important point is that:

*"IBM Planning Analytics enables users to discover insights automatically, directly from their data, and drive decision-making with the predictive capabilities of **IBM Watson Analytics**. It also incorporates scorecards and dashboards to monitor KPIs and communicate business results through a variety of visualizations"*

- (IBM.com)

So, the key objective of this chapter's project is to use Watson Analytics to (hopefully) improve on a user-created (in Planning Analytics) forecast. We will use Watson Analytics to explore sales data at a deeper level with rich visualizations and identify new insights on the available product performance data.

Our data

So, in our organization, financial analysts must supply *projections* for values for forecasts on each product revenue, which is also *broken down* by retailer country, order method, and period.

In Planning Analytics, there is a multi-dimensional cube defined with the following dimensionality:

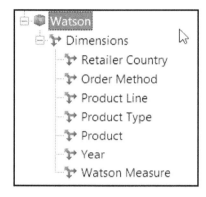

Using the **extract, transform, and load** (ETL) tool that is native to Planning Analytics (known as **TurboIntegrator**), product performance information such as quantities sold and revenue is automatically loaded on a schedule from the organization's general ledger system into the Planning Analytics cube at the end of each and every business day.

Analysts use Excel-based *linked* worksheets to view product performance information or can use the Planning Analytics **Cube Viewer** to view detailed information for the products they own or are responsible for creating a forecast for:

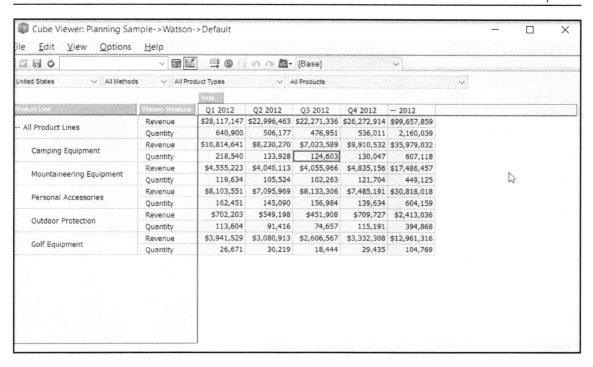

The Planning Analytics cube is *memory-based*, and so an analyst can slice and dice the data in any number of ways and the numbers will be recalculated and/or consolidated in real-time, helping the analyst better understand the results. The preceding data view is **Revenue** and **Quantity** for the **United States**, **All Methods**, **All Product Types**, and **All Products**, but broken down by Product Line, across periods (at the quarter level).

Another view—or slice—of the data may be **Revenue**, year-over-year by **Retailer Country**:

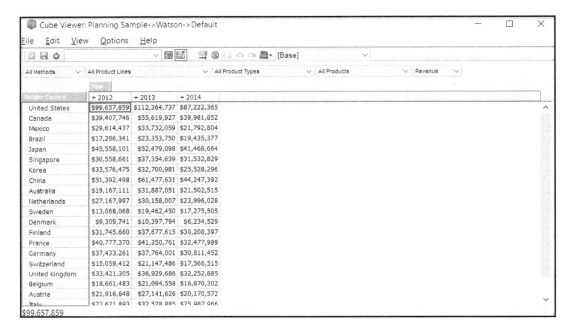

Another useful feature provided by Planning Analytics is its ability to dynamically chart most of the views you create using data in the Planning Analytics cube, by using the cube viewer:

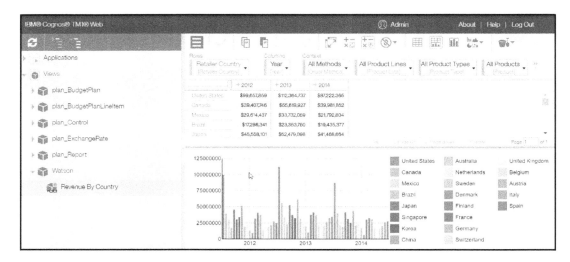

Creating the forecast

Every analyst has access to historic sales information for products in Planning Analytics and can create various views (and charts) of the data, similar to the ones shown in the previous section, as well as any offline, perhaps intangible knowledge they may come across from the media or other sources. In other words, the forecaster looks at detailed reports (views), showing how much of the product was sold in previous years for the forecast period and makes assumptions as to how differently the product will sell in the same period in the future.

You can see that using Planning Analytics to gain knowledge about data is an advantage, but there is an opportunity here to leverage Watson Analytics to further improve this process.

In the next section, we will create a Watson Analytics project using the same data stored in our Planning Analytics cube to dig deeper into the product data.

Starting the project

To proceed with our project, we need to get the data *out* of the Planning Analytic cube and into Watson Analytics. To do this, there are several options. First, we could use the Planning Analytics ETL tool again, this time to export data to a **comma-delimited** (**CSV**) file or, since this is an initial exploration of the process, we can also simply right-click on our cube view and select **Export as Text Data...**:

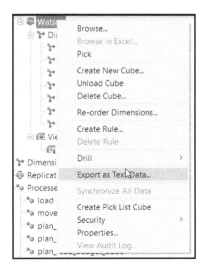

Note: When using Watson Analytics, you can also import data using a data connection rather than using a raw file upload such as an XLS, XLSX, CSV, SAV file. Watson Analytics offers many data connectors that can be used to import various forms of data. The list of available data connectors is ever-increasing as the development team continues to implement new connectors to suit the needs of their customers (IBM Product Documentation).

Once we have our file of data (a portion of it is shown in the following screenshot, opened in MS Excel), we can use the **+Add** feature on the Watson Analytics Welcome page to upload the file to Watson Analytics:

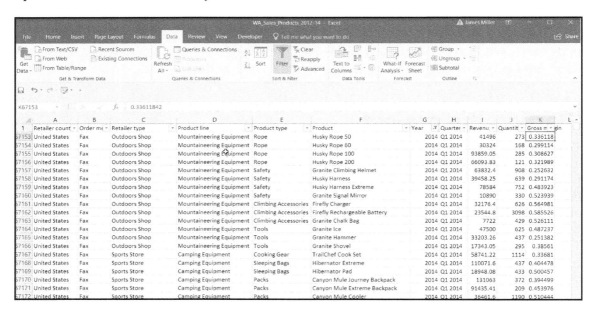

Our data has now been loaded into Watson Analytics, like so:

Developing the project

Once again, with the objective of becoming more intimate with our data, we can use the **Explore** feature in Watson Analytics to have Watson suggest to us various interesting starting points:

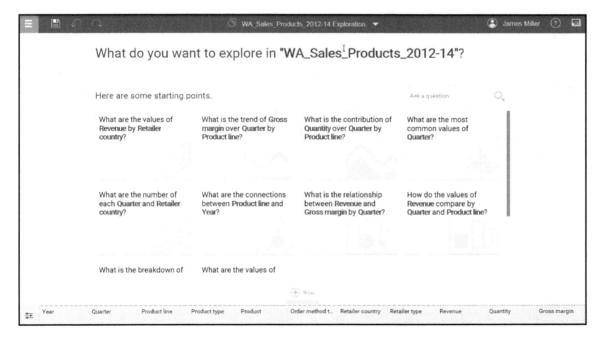

Although Planning Analytics provides us with a way to view **Revenue** by **Retailer Country**, it requires us to create a report (or view) of the data using the cube viewer and is in a common row and column format. We could also experiment with the charting feature, but here we can see that Watson Analytics automatically generated a neat, easy-to-comprehend visualization on the data automatically:

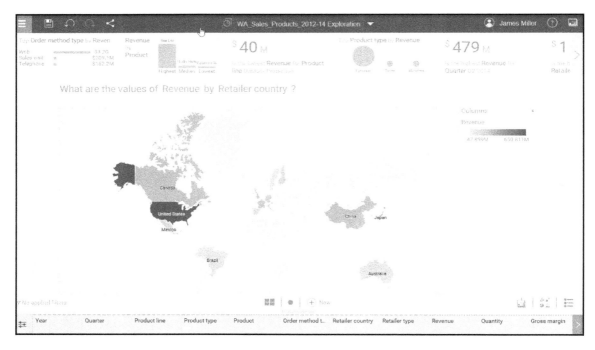

Viewing Revenue by Retailer Country

Keep in mind that the Watson Analytics visualizations are dynamic, drillable, and provide out of the box context sensitivity:

The other report view that we created earlier in this chapter (using the Planning Analytics cube viewer) was the **Revenue by Product Line** view over quarters.

The following screenshot shows that same information, which was created by Watson Analytics automatically for us:

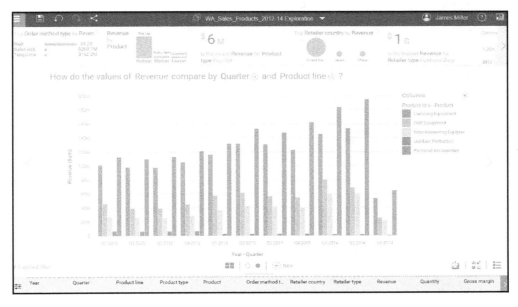

View of Revenue by Product Line

As we continue to explore our data using Watson Analytics, we can again go to the insights provided across the top of each page for more knowledge.

For example, Watson Analytics provides our **Top Product Type by Revenue**:

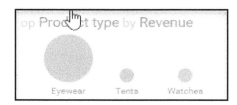

Clicking on that insight and selecting **+ New Page**, we will see the following visualization generated for us on a new page:

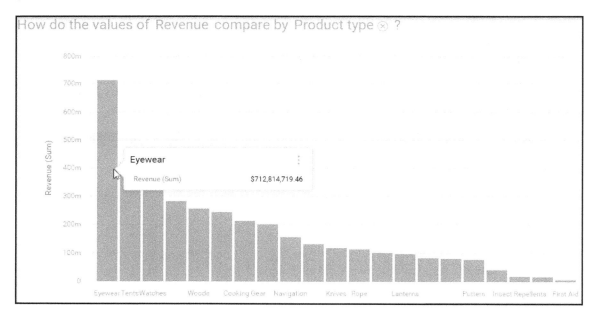

Based upon revenues, it would seem that **Eyewear** is the **Top Product Type**.

I wonder—how (what *order method*) do we sell the most of this type of product? To answer that question, we can click on the visualization and select **Show by** and **Order method type**:

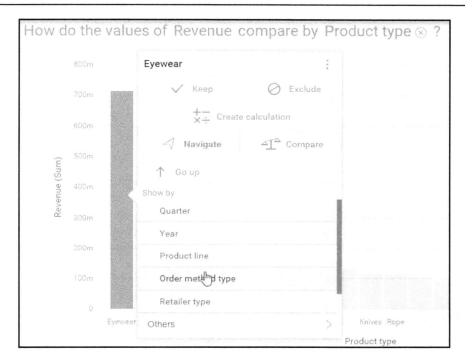

Watson Analytics automatically shows us that online purchases (the web) is the most common method of purchasing our **Eyewear** product type (during this time period):

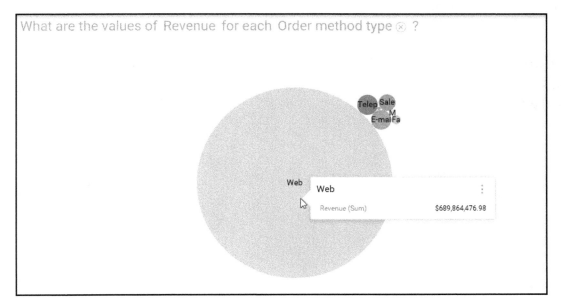

Note that for the preceding visualization, I have used the Visualization Types icon (as shown in the following screenshot) to change the visualization type to a bubble Chart:

To change the type, you can choose from a list of Watson Analytics *recommended* visualizations, or you can choose one of the other types. In this way, Watson makes sure that you use the visualization type that will be the most comprehensive, based upon the data question you have selected or created. If you choose to experiment, keep in mind that, depending on the visualization type that you choose, the visualization might be empty because there are required data items that are undefined.

Visualizations and data requirements

Visualization types each have their own precise requirements for displaying data correctly. For example, a bar chart requires one `category` column and one value or `measure` column. There is a full list describing each type's requirement within the Watson online documentation if you search for *visualization types*. It is worth a few minutes to familiarize yourself with these details.

More questioning

In addition to the top product types (which we reviewed earlier in this section), we can look at the **Top Products** just as easily:

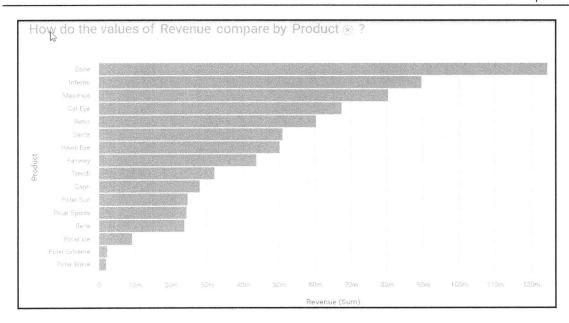

With the preceding visualization, we are only looking at the **Top Products**.

The following screenshot shows the visualization that was created by comparing **Revenue** by **All Products**; perhaps not as useful (since there are so many products ?

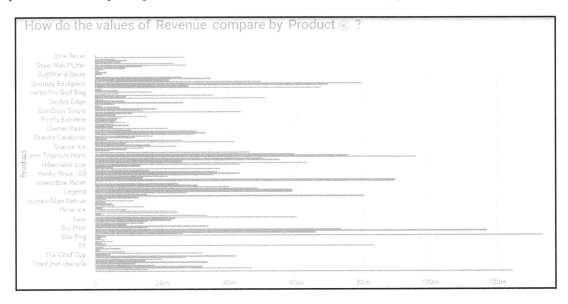

As a forecaster, we are most likely not interested in forecasting all of the products (although there may be some value in reviewing all product performance). What we can do from the preceding visualization is make some dynamic modifications to it to show only those products that we may be responsible for. Go through the following steps in order to understand this better:

1. If we click on the visualization where it says **Columns**, we can then select **Product** (you can see in the following image that all **144** products are currently included in the visualization):

2. From there, let's click on **Set a condition**:

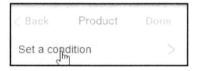

3. Next, type in `putter` and click **Apply**:

4. Watson Analytics then updates our visualization in real-time, showing the revenue on three golfing products (the **Blue Steel Max Putter**, the **Blue Steel Putter**, and the **Course Pro Putter**):

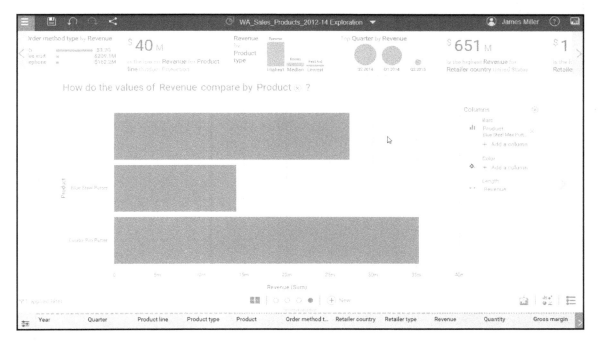

Viewing Revenue of three golfing products: Blue Steel Max Putter, Steel Putter, and Course Pro Putter

Time Series

Earlier in this chapter, we mentioned common forecasting methods. One popular approach uses Time Series analysis to identify trends. When asking questions about data, **trend** is a very important keyword. By creating a question in Watson Analytics, you can have Watson use line visualizations to help you identify trends in the data. This would be of value in our Time Series forecasts.

To illustrate this, we can (for example) use the following question in Watson Analytics:

What is the trend of Gross margin over Quarter ⊗ by Product line ⊗ ?

Which will generate the following visualization:

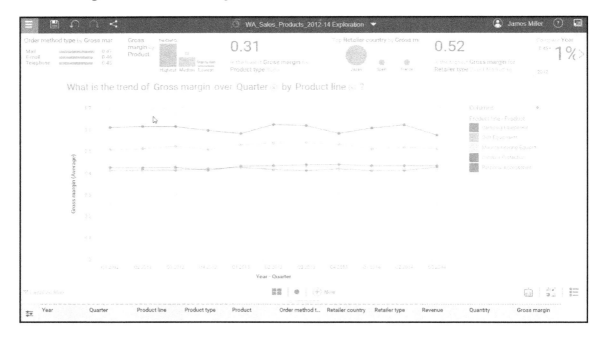

View of Gross margin using Product line

Of course, it is very easy to filter the visualization by clicking on a **Product line** listed on the right-hand side of the page:

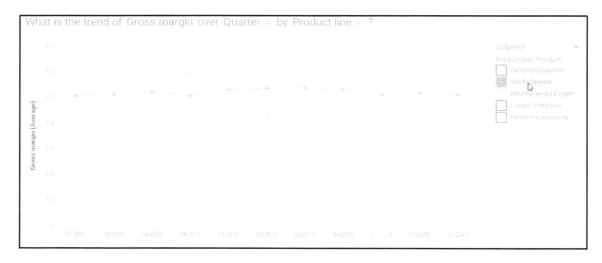

If we click on the word **Product line** in the question, we can easily change **Product line** to
Product:

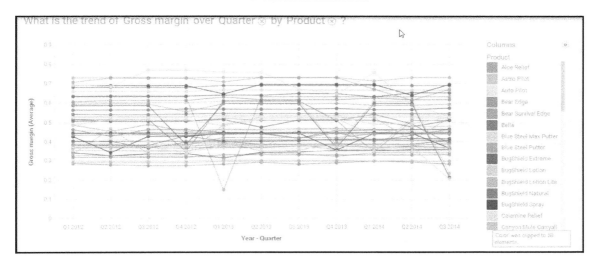

And then, like before, filter the products to the three *golfing products* we want to see:

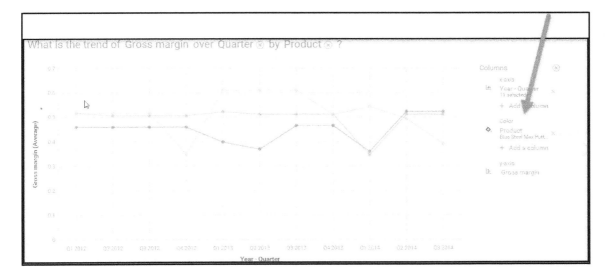

In the preceding screenshot, we can see the visualization that Watson Analytics has generated to show the trend of **Gross margin** on our favorite three products, quarter by quarter. However, we are forecasting *Revenue*, so let's change **Gross margin** to **Revenue** (by clicking on the word **Gross margin** and selecting **Revenue**):

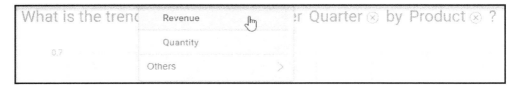

Now, Watson Analytics updates our visualization again for us:

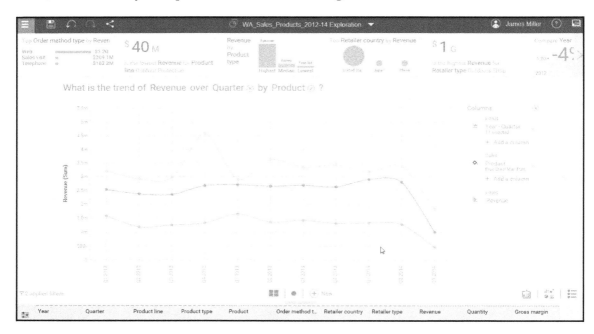

Changing Gross margin to Revenue

Other visualization options

You can always click on the Visualizations Options icon in the lower right of the page (as shown in the following screenshot) to make some additional changes to the current visualization. In this example, I have checked **Show labels vertically** and also checked **Smooth lines**.

Smoothing is a process that levels out fluctuations in the actual data to represent the overall trend a bit better. In other words, it *makes the line between data points curved*. If not selected, straight lines are used to connect data points:

Another view of the same visualization is shown in the following screenshot, with the title, grid lines, and axis turned off. You may want to experiment with these options if you plan to add the visualization to a presentation later and do not need the textual references, and so on:

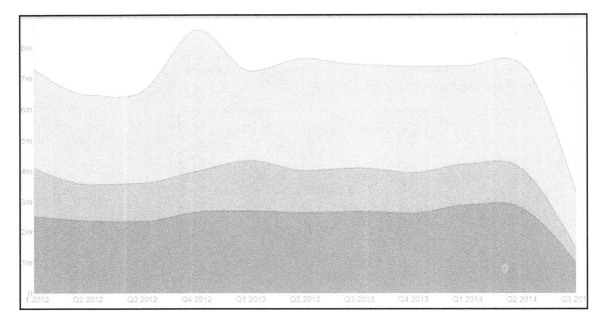

So, now that we have explored and experimented enough with our data, let's move on to the more formal results review phase of the project.

Reviewing the results

Finally, at this stage in the project, we should have already created and reviewed a reasonable number of visualizations, and hopefully gained insights not previously known that will help us prepare a more accurate product revenue forecast.

In this project, we might not be so interested in sharing assets with colleagues as much as wanting to just use the information and insights gained in creating the product forecast we are responsible for. To that point, we most likely would *not* use the Watson Analytics **Assemble** features (as we have done in previous chapter projects).

Although we might not use **Assemble**, the **Exploration** can be saved so that we can keep those views and visualizations that we feel are valuable enough to us and that we can use regularly to prepare future forecasts. The following is a simple example.

If we have asked the following question:

What is the contribution of Revenue over Product ⊗ by Quarter ⊗ ?

Watson Analytics will generate the following visualization:

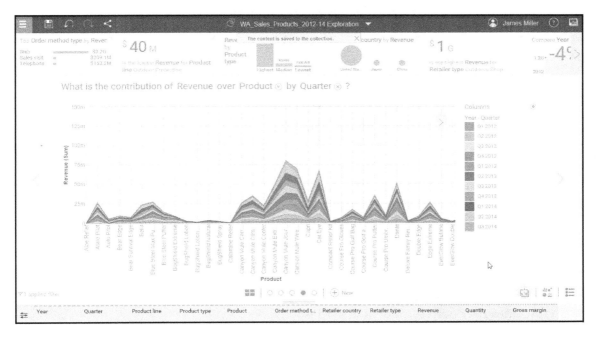

View to Revenue by Product for each Quarter

If we've saved our **Exploration**, the view is saved as part of that Exploration. Notice in the view that we can see the **Revenue** by **Product** for each quarter in our data (**Q1 2012** through **Q3 2014**).

Now, suppose that at some time in the future we have a new extract file from our Planning Analytics cube that includes more data, for more periods. We can update or enhance the data that is in that dataset by simply replacing the data that it contains.

When you replace the data in a dataset, the predictions, explorations, and views that are based on that dataset are automatically updated. You can add or delete columns and rows or change the existing data. To refresh the data, you can do the following:

1. On the Welcome page, find the dataset whose data you want to replace and click on it.
2. Click **Replace all data.**
3. Select your dataset.
4. Close any open message boxes when your data upload is complete:

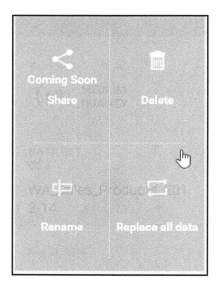

Now, if we reopen our saved **Exploration** and look at that same visualization, we can see that it includes new periods of data in the visualization:

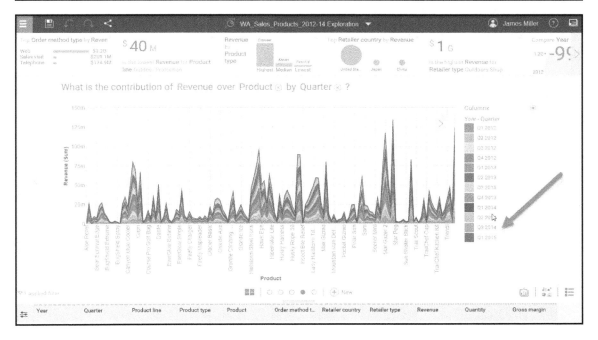

View to exploration with new periods of data

Summary

In this chapter, a Watson Analytics project was used to test product forecasting performance; it was created by analysts using IBM Planning Analytics. We created an extract file from the Planning Analytics cube and loaded it into Watson Analytics. From there, we used Watson's Explore functionality to examine the data and gain insights that can help us better understand our data and hopefully create a more accurate product revenue forecast. We also saved the Exploration, refreshed our data, and reused the Explorations saved visualizations with the updated data.

In the next chapter, we will use **Artificial Intelligence** (**AI**) from a Watson perspective in order to walk through an example use-case project that relates to the banking industry, in which transactions are evaluated to identify fraud.

Anomaly Detection in Banking Using AI

9

This chapter will look at the process of anomaly detection from a Watson Analytics perspective, walking through an example use case project relative in to the banking industry in which transactions are evaluated to identify potentially fraudulent situations.

This chapter will cover the following topics:

- Defining the problem
- Starting the project
- Developing the project
- Reviewing the results

Defining the problem

In data mining, anomaly detection (or outlier detection) is defined as the identification of items, events, or observations that do not conform to an expected pattern (or other items) in a dataset, and that are sometimes referred to as **rare events**. These events raise suspicion and, typically, the anomalous items will translate to some kind of problem that requires deeper attention and needs to be addressed. Common events include bank fraud, structural defects, medical conditions, or simply mistakes in a text.

 Anomalous items that raise suspicions by differing significantly from the majority of the data may also be referred to as outliers, novelties, noise, deviations, and exceptions.

Anomaly detection is a technique or method that is used to identify unusual patterns that don't seem to conform to the accepted behavior. You will routinely see anomaly detection techniques used in many areas such as intrusion detection, system-health monitoring, and fraud detection.

No matter what the application might be, it is critical to first establish and understand certain baselines and boundaries that will define what an anomaly is (for that application).

Anomalies are generally categorized as point (which is when a single data point is too different from then most others), contextual (contextual anomalies are only a problem in specific situations/contexts), or collective (when data as part of a set becomes an issue anomalies).

It's important to grasp that the process of anomaly detection is comparable to noise removal and novelty detection, but novelty detection is the process of identifying an unobserved pattern in new observations that are not included in the training data, while noise removal is the process of removing the occurrence of unwanted observations from the meaningful data.

Banking use cases

As we have already mentioned, anomaly detection enjoys a wide range of use cases. However, in this chapter, we have chosen to focus on those relating to the banking industry, and specifically, fraud detection.

Banking-related fraud schemes are typically categorized into areas that include corruption, cash, billing, check tampering, skimming, larceny, and financial statement deception.

Corruption

A Simple example of corruption detection in banks would be identifying transactions that include customers who appear on the **US Treasury Department Office of Foreign Asset Control (OFAC)** list, or those organizations on the list of uncooperative countries and territories.

Cash

Fraudulent cash scheme detection is all about looking for events that are outside of a previously established baseline, for example, those cash transactions that are slightly below regulatory reporting thresholds, or a succession of cash disbursements by a customer number that together exceed regulatory reporting thresholds, or statistically unusual numbers of cash transfers by a particular customer or bank account.

Billing

Billing fraud detection focuses on the process of identifying a remarkably large number of fees waived by a branch or an employee. Again, what constitutes "remarkably large" is determined by historic activities or previously established baselines.

Check tampering

The occurrence of check tampering can be identified from the occurrence of missing, duplicate, void, or outofsequence check numbers, checks paid that do not match checks issued, by bank or by check, within a stated period of time.

Skimming

Skimming activities can be highlighted by very short term deposits and withdrawals on the same account, as well as duplicate checks or credit card transactions.

Larceny

Larceny detection involves the identification of certain kinds of events, such as a number of loans taken by a certain customer or bank employee without any payments or reimbursements applied to them, or loan amounts that are greater than the value of their stated collateral. Additional larceny flags include sudden activities in dormant accounts.

Financial statement fraud

Finally, financial statement fraud detection involves the monitoring of otherwise dormant and suspended **general ledger** (**GL**) accounts as well as **journal entries** (**JEs**) made at suspicious times.

The preceding descriptions are only a short list of fraud examples, and new methods for committing bank fraud are being introduced each year. According to Ernst and Young, more than 500 million checks are forged annually, with losses totaling more than $10 billion. You can see why understanding the concept of anomaly detection is critically important.

Starting the project

Now, that we have established a bit of background information as to the definition of the various types of banking fraud, we can begin this chapter's projects, starting with a review of the data we'll be working with.

The project in this chapter is focused on identifying fraudulent transactions.

Our data will be a file of transactions that have been made at a particular bank over a period of time. Since the type of fraud we are interested in involves comparing transactions to a normal amount (of the transaction or activity), as part of the project, we will need to understand what the cash baseline should be.

In the past, the Currency and Foreign Transactions Reporting Act (established in 1970) introduced the requirement that banks need to report all suspicious currency transactions. The intent of this requirement was to prevent tax evasion and money laundering by criminals who used cash deposits to disguise the illegal source of their funds. The law stipulates that the transactions that need to be reported include those that total more than $10,000 in a single deposit, or if the bank receives multiple payments from the same agent or individual over the course of a year adding up to more than $10,000.

Banks are also required to report smaller transactions that may be a sign of suspicious activity. For example, guidelines say that suspicious activity could include a deposit or withdrawal of $5,000 or more by a customer who doesn't normally make transactions that are that large.

Furthermore, we will also look for evidence of check tempering in our file of transactions, such as examining the cashed or canceled check numbers, searching for missing, duplicate, void, or outofsequence numbers.

There are a variety of other guidelines and requirements that banking institutions need to adhere to, but for this project, since we are focusing on cash and check fraud, we can move on here and have a quick look at the raw data file provided for the project.

The data

The data that we will look at for this chapter's project comes to us in the form of a bank transaction report file, and is comprised of a set of records that provide detailed information on the transactions recorded in the **bank's reconciliation** (**BR**) process.

The fields in the data file include the following:

- **Transaction Code**
- **Transaction Date**
- **Cancellation Date**
- **Transaction Number**
- **Check Number**
- **Deposit Number**
- **Payee Name/Description**
- **Reference Number**
- **Currency Code**
- **Bank Number**
- **Reference Number**
- **Outstanding Balance**
- **Canceled Amount**

The following screenshot shows a page from a sample report generated from similar set of data:

05/11/07 11:57:12 AM					National Office Supply USA				Page 1 of 1
Printed By: Supervisor					**BR Transaction Listing**				

Trs Code	Trs Date	Cnl Date	Trans #	Check #	Deposit # Payee Name/Desc	Reference	Outstanding	Cancelled
Bank #: BOFA-C1 (Bank of America - Payroll)					Currency Code: USD (Dollars)			
CHECKBOOK	05/11/07		1000000006		Checkbook costs		-500.00	
CHECKBOOK	05/11/07		1000000007		others		-850.00	
TRANSFER	05/11/07		1000000001		Transfer		5,000.00	
TRANSFER	05/11/07		1000000002		Transfer		2,000.00	
TRANSFER	05/11/07		1000000003		Replenishment		1,000.00	
TRANSFER	05/11/07		1000000004		Transfer		450.00	
TRANSFER	05/11/07		1000000005		Transfer		300.00	
BOFA-C1: 7 Record(s)					Total for BOFA-C1: USD		7,400.00	0.00
Bank #: CHASE (Chase Manhattan Bank)					Currency Code: USD (Dollars)			
CHECKBOOK	05/11/07	05/11/07	1000000006		Other charges			-600.00
DEPOSIT	01/15/07	01/25/07	1000000001		100001 Investment deposit	Transfer ticket #125		1,000,000.00
TRANSFER	01/25/07	05/11/07	1000000002		Replenishment of funds	DM # 15654500012		-50,000.00
TRANSFER	05/11/07	05/11/07	1000000003		Transfer			-2,000.00
TRANSFER	05/11/07		1000000004		Transfer		3,200.00	
TRANSFER	05/11/07		1000000005		Transfer		500.00	
CHASE: 6 Record(s)					Total for CHASE: USD		3,700.00	947,400.00
Bank #: CITIBANK (Citibank Corporation)					Currency Code: USD (Dollars)			
CHARGES	01/21/07	01/23/07	1000000002	5002	Citibank	DM # 101256262		-150.00
CHECKBOOK	05/11/07	05/11/07	1000000009		Checkbook costs			-900.00
DEPOSIT	05/11/07		1000000005		10004 Deposits		7,500.00	
DEPOSIT	05/11/07	05/11/07	1000000006		10005 Deposits			3,600.00
DEPOSIT	01/21/07		1000000001		10001 Cash Deposits from	CM # 100052563	15,263.25	
DEPOSIT	05/11/07		1000000003		10002 Deposits		2,500.00	
DEPOSIT	05/11/07		1000000004		10003 Deposits		5,400.00	
INCOME	05/11/07	05/11/07	1000000008		Receipts			600.00
TRANSFER	05/11/07	05/11/07	1000000007		Transfer			-1,200.00
CITIBANK: 9 Record(s)					Total for CITIBANK: USD		30,663.25	1,950.00
Report: 22 Record(s)					Total for this Report: USD		41,763.25	949,350.00

Sample report generated

To get a quick peek of our raw data, we can open the data file using Microsoft Excel. A portion of the file is shown in the following screenshot:

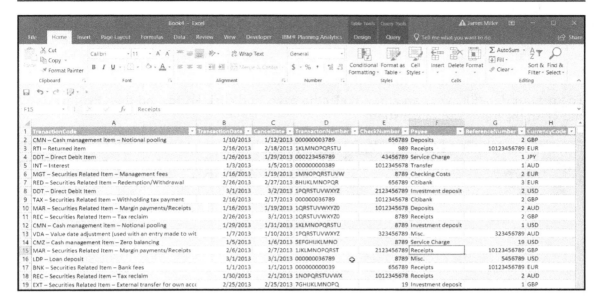

Even when using Microsoft Excel, we can see that there are many types of bank transactions found within our project data, and each transaction is assigned a **business transaction code** (**BTC**) that identifies the transaction's purpose.

This transaction code will make it easier to look at only cash-related transitions in an effort to find those transactions that may be a part of a fraud scheme. Other interesting and important fields or columns of data include the **Bank ID**, **Check Number**, and **Canceled Amount**.

On to starting the project.

Developing the project

Once again, once we have obtained the data in the form of a file in this case, our file of bank transactions and have performed our initial data review, we will need to load the file into Watson Analytics, using the usual method from the **Welcome** page (**+Add**, then **Upload data**).

Once the data has been loaded, we can proceed to the next step in the project, which is usually to begin using Watson Analytics **Explore** function.

As we have explained in previous chapters, you can use **Explore** to ask questions about data (and build interactive visualizations) quite easily. You can also create, filter, and explore multiple visualizations of the data to try to discover patterns and relationships in the data.

To load our data file, we start at the **Welcome** page, and click **+Add,** and then **Explore** as shown in the following screenshot:

Next, we select our `BankTransactions` file from the list, as shown in the following screenshot:

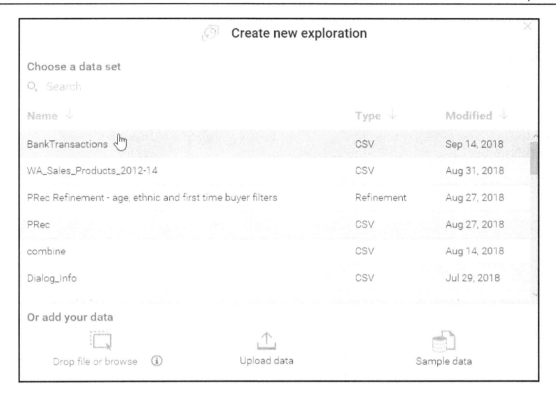

Once again, as we've seen in earlier chapters of this book, with **Explore**, you can use the language and keywords that you feel are most related to the objectives of your project to come up with questions that then help you to explore and visualize the data you are analyzing.

In our earlier projects, we have seen that Watson Analytics uses worded questions rather than programming code or queries to generate a list of starting points that you can read through, and then use them to create visualizations that meet your project's requirements. With Watson Analytics, it is really all about developing the right questions rather than a structured query syntax.

The first question

This chapter's project focuses on identifying situations of possible check fraud. As we have seen, one redflag event that auditors usually look for is a canceled amount (cashed checks) that is outside of what is considered normal for a particular bank account.

With this idea in mind, having previously reviewed our project's data and become familiar with the data columns within the file, we can start asking our first question, with the focus on the following data columns:

- **CanceledAmount**
- **CheckNumber**

Perhaps our first question might be *how do the values of* **CanceledAmount** *compare by* **CheckNumber**? It is shown in the screenshot:

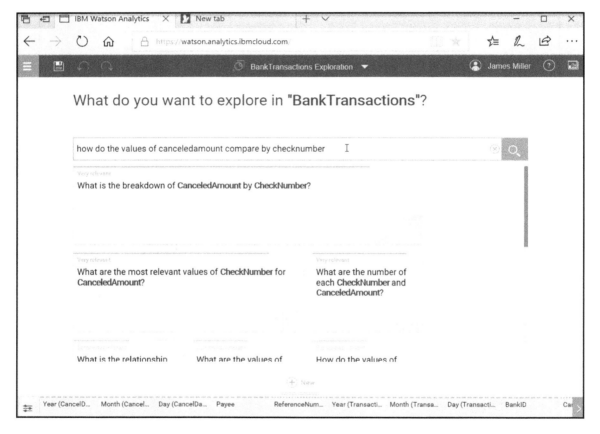

This seems like an appropriate question for us to ask our data, since it is similar to a structured query that you might run on a relational database, such as the following:

```
Select checknumber, canceledamount order by checknumber
```

Using such a database query, the results would be returned in a format that is more tabular in nature.

Using Excel for sorting and filtering the data

Another approach to performing our analysis that might come to mind is by sorting and filtering the data using Microsoft Excel.

Since Microsoft Excel is a well-known and popular tool, before we look at any visualizations that are generated as a result of asking our questions in Watson Analytics, let's take a moment here to look at the same data (and question) using Microsoft Excel.

The following screenshot shows that even with the columns **CheckNumber** and **CanceledAmount** highlighted in yellow—more analysis is required before we can find any insights:

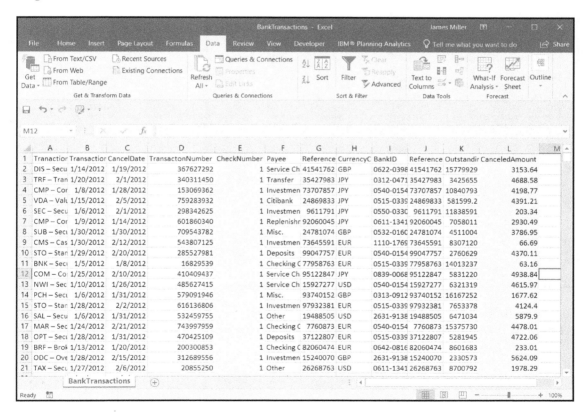

The first thing that we should realize here is that we need to group the data by the **Bank ID** column, if we want to see what the normal or average canceled amount is for each **Bank ID**, since the normal amount for each bank is most likely different to what the average is for all bank IDs.

Think about it: Each of the bank IDs most likely have higher daily averages because they are used for different purposes.

In Microsoft Excel, we could add a **filter** (shown in the following screenshot) on the **Bank ID** column, but it still isn't much help:

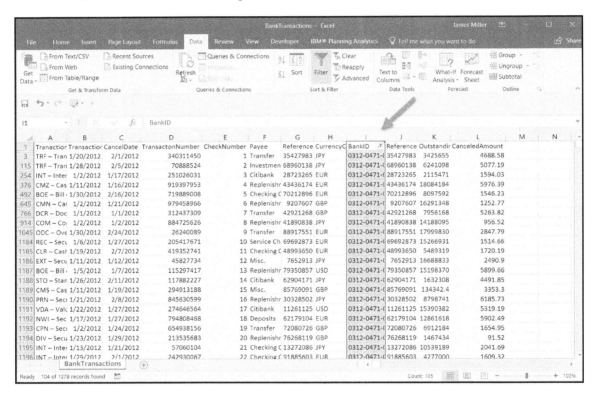

To be fair, there are other Microsoft Excel approaches to performing this analysis, but let's get back to Watson Analytics and see what it can do for us.

Back to Watson

If we look at the first Watson Analytics visualization that was based upon our original question, we see the following:

This visualization, although perhaps prettier, is not much more helpful than the Microsoft Excel result we looked at earlier, but we can see quite easily that there is a somewhat larger variance in the canceled amounts for each check.

This observation wasn't as obvious when we were using Microsoft Excel, looking at rows and columns of our data. Now, if we add a filter on the bank ID to our Watson visualization, we can really see something that may be considered somewhat suspicious, as shown in the following screenshot:

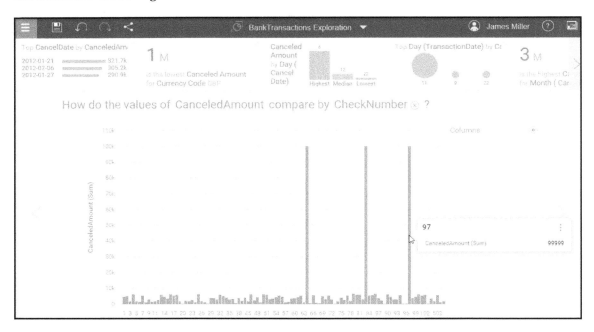

In this visualization that is automatically generated for us by Watson Analytics, it is easy to see that there are three canceled amounts that are found during this period that are *much larger* than what we can see is the normal amount for this particular bank ID. Hovering over those checks shows us the check number and amount, showing that all three amounts are the same $9,999.

From here, we can continue the analysis of our data by asking some additional questions, such as how do the values of **CanceledAmount** compare by bank ID?

The resulting visualization, shown in the following screenshot, proves to us that the previous visualization has highlighted several transactions involving amounts that are out of what is considered normal for this bank ID, in that it shows the average canceled amounts by bank ID, and our highlighted bank ID (**0312-0471-0**) has an average of only $6,000:

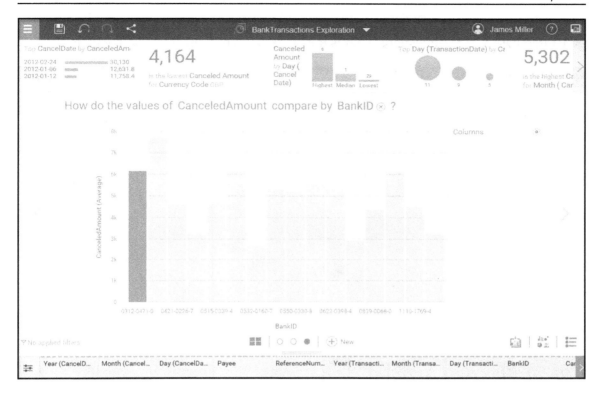

Check numbers

Another red flag, or audit point, for us to look for within our data is check numbers that are out of sequence. Typically, an account will have check transactions showing check numbers that are canceled or cashed in order, as an individual or accountant will use the next check number by habit in an effort to keep proper records.

If the check numbers drawn for a particular bank ID, during a short period of time, are found to be more than a few numbers out of the current sequence, it is classified as a suspicious event.

Watson Analytics can help us with this analysis as well. The following is a visualization generated based on the question: What is the breakdown of **BankID** and **CheckNumber**?

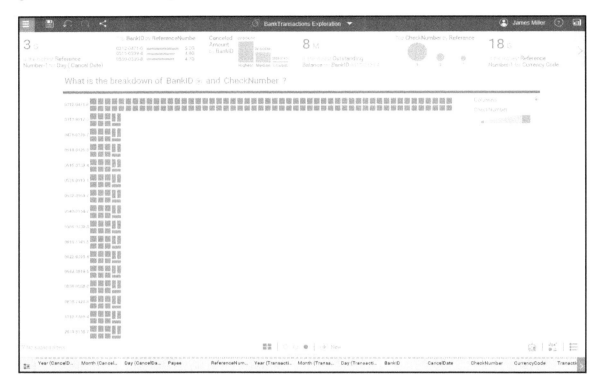

Excluding data, with a quick glance, the first **BankID** (**0312-0471-0**) in the visualization seems interesting (in that it has a longer list number of canceled checks). In Watson Analytics, we can click on the **Visualization Content** section (to the right of the page), select on the row, and then unselect all of the BankIDs from the list (except for the first one), as shown in the following screenshot:

Now we have a more focused visualization to study, as shown in the following screenshot:

After studying the preceding Watson Analytics visualization, we can zoom into the check number matrix and see that there are four check numbers (**501**, **502**, **503**, and **504**) that are outside of the current sequence of 1 through 104, as shown in the following screenshot:

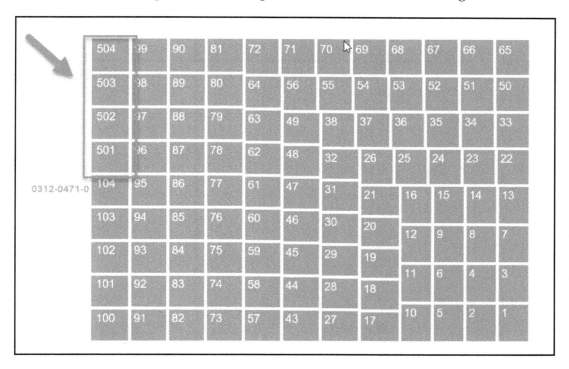

Suppose someone still wants to see the data in a row and column format? Well, Watson Analytics allows for that as well. In the following visualization, we have asked the question `how does BankID relate to CheckNumber for CanceledAmount?`:

With the results, we have then clicked on the **Visualization types** icon as shown in the following screenshot:

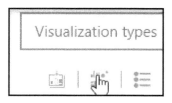

We have then changed the visualization type to **Grid,** as shown in the following screenshot:

Using a **Grid** type of visualization, we can see the check numbers in sequence, as well as each check's canceled amount. If we scroll vertically through the check numbers, we will again see the check numbers that seem to be out of sequence or out of the expected ordering, as shown in the following screenshot:

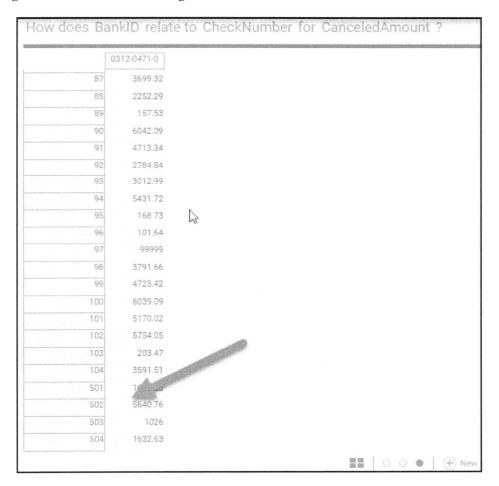

Just to be sure that the check numbers (**501**, **502**, **503**, and **504**) *are* out of the expected order (that is, what happened to check numbers 105 through 500?), we might want to see what dates these checks were cashed or canceled on. To do that, we can return to our grid visualization and click on the **Visualization Content** section to the right of the grid (shown in the following screenshot), then click on **+ Add Column** to find, select, and add the data column **CanceledDate**:

Adding CanceledDate column

Once we have done that, our grid visualization will include the date that each check was cashed on, all presented in a rows and columns format as shown in the following screenshot:

How does BankID relate to CheckNumber ⊗ for CanceledAmount ?

		0312-0471-0
87	2012-02-02	3699.32
88	2012-02-01	2252.29
89	2012-02-09	157.53
90	2012-01-22	6042.09
91	2012-01-17	4713.34
92	2012-02-06	2784.84
93	2012-01-19	3012.99
94	2012-01-13	5431.72
95	2012-01-14	168.73
96	2012-02-06	101.64
97	2012-01-15	99999
98	2012-02-15	3791.66
99	2012-02-01	4723.42
100	2012-01-18	6039.09
101	2012-02-18	5170.02
102	2012-02-05	5754.05
103	2012-01-31	203.47
104	2012-01-30	3591.51
501	2012-02-14	1612.25
502	2012-01-25	5640.76
503	2012-01-26	1026
504	2012-02-01	1632.63

New

Reviewing the results

When reviewing the results of your Watson Analytics project analysis, Watson Analytics can use many visualization methods to display the results of the analysis of the data you are interested in. It is imperative that you take the time to begin to understand and feel comfortable with the definitions of the visualization types as they apply to Watson Analytics.

The types currently supported by Watson Analytics include: bar chart, bubble plot, classification accuracy table, density plot, difference graph, heat map, histogram, marginal distribution visualization, packed bubble visualization, pie chart, prediction table, scatter plot, tree diagram and tree map – all of which are described very well in the Watson Analytics product documentation and is a good use of the readers time to review.

Collecting

Once again, as we work with any data in Watson Analytics, you can (and should) set aside interesting or important visualizations that you acquire from using **Explore**, **Predict**, and **Assemble**. As you work with Watson Analytics, you should get into the habit of clicking the **Collect** icon (as shown in the following screenshot) as often as possible:

It is always better to overcollect and sort out the saved visualizations later than have to recreate something from scratch from your data.

Telling the story

Once you have your collection started by saving the various visualizations you have chosen during analysis, the next step is to use Watson Analytics' **Assemble** functionality to gather the most relevant visualizations that you feel are best to help tell your story or get your point across.

For example, in this chapter's project, we can perform the following steps:

1. From the Watson Analytics **Welcome** page, click on **Assemble** and then select our project's `BankTransactions` file, as shown in the following screenshot:

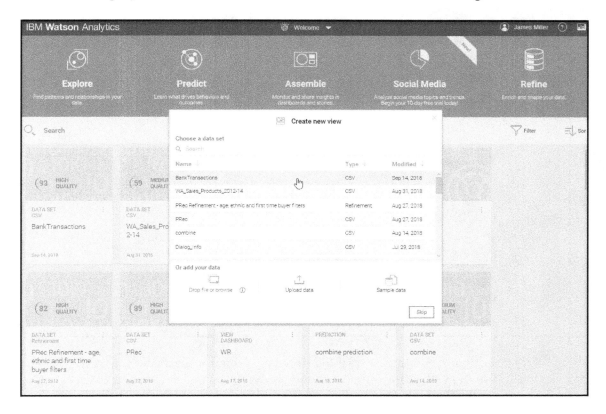

2. From this point, we can enter a name for our **View**, then select **Single page** (in the **Dashboard**) and then the single, blank page layout, as shown in the following screenshot:

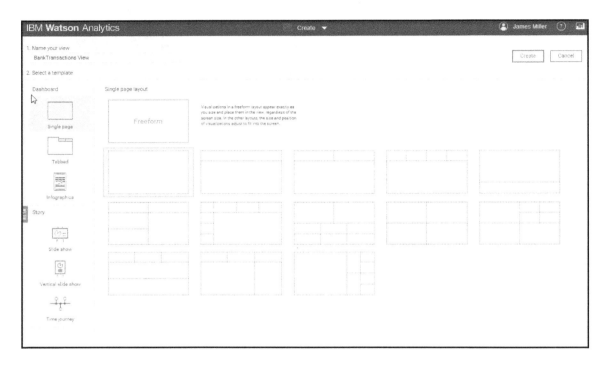

3. Rather than recreating or tracking down a relevant visualization, we can then click on the **Collection** icon (as shown in the following screenshot) to access and view our collection:

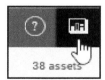

4. Finally, once we determine the saved visualizations that we want to use, we can simply drag and drop those saved visualizations onto the page, as shown in the following screenshot:

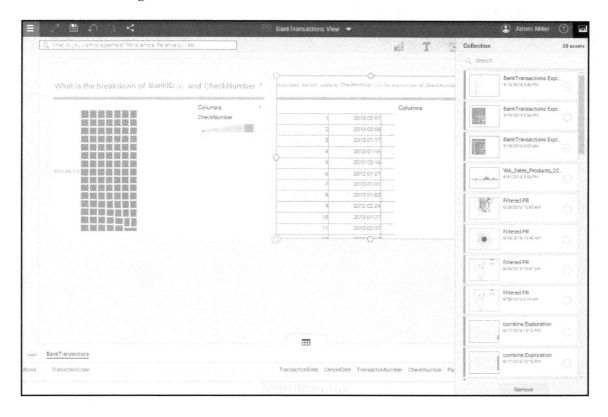

5. At this point, you can use the many features of Assemble to create and set aside visualizations and other items to reuse in other dashboards and stories that you create. When you are finished (or if you are finished for now), you can click on the **Save** icon to store your masterpiece, as shown in the following screenshot:

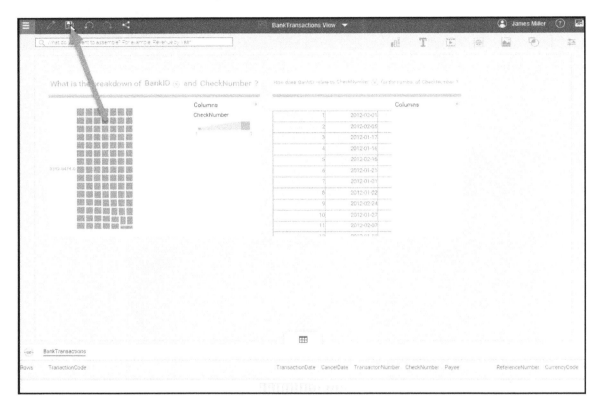

6. Once you click **Save**, you can assign a name so that you can share or continue editing the view at a later time:

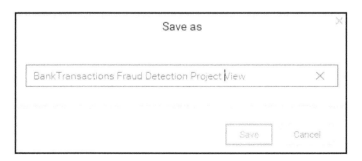

7. The following image shows the **Welcome** page with our new view saved and ready for reuse, as shown in the following screenshot:

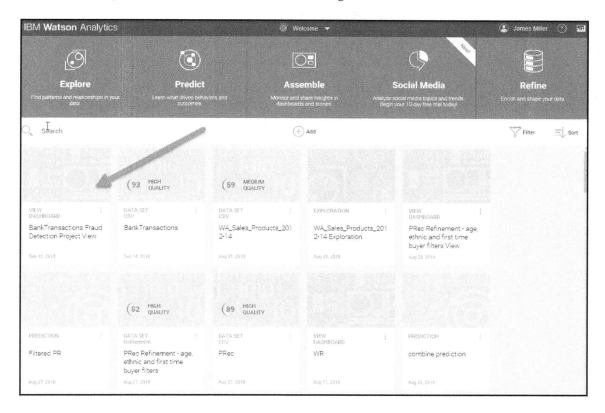

Summary

In this chapter, we looked at the process of anomaly detection using Watson Analytics by using an example use case project set in to the banking industry, in which we used Watson's Explore functionality to examine bank transactions to identify possible fraud. We also compared various formats and tools during the analysis process.

The next chapter will be a global summary of what you have learned through the previous chapters and what you can do next to continue the Watson Analytics learning process.

10 What's Next

This being the final chapter of our book, we will offer a chapter-by-chapter comprehensive summary as well as what we have (hopefully) learned through the use case projects in this book, and finally, what you can do next to continue with the IBM Watson Analytics learning process.

The breakdown of this chapter is simply:

- Chapter-by-chapter summary
- Suggested next steps

Chapter-by-chapter summary

The following sections contain the final review of each chapter along with some key takeaways from each.

Chapter 1 – The Essentials of IBM Watson

In our first chapter, we defined (the latest version of) IBM Watson Analytics as well as offered various objectives for the tool. We also provided an overview of Watson Analytics' current interface, pointing out its major components. A refresher on performing basic tasks in Watson Analytics (such as adding data, exploring data, and creating a prediction) was also given.

The following are the key takeaways:

- IBM Watson was named after IBM's first CEO and industrialist, Thomas J. Watson and the term **Cognitive** is defined as *concerned with the act or process of knowing or perceiving*.
- IBM Watson lives in the IBM cloud, which makes it relatively easy to get started using Watson Analytics.

- The IBM Cloud platform is where you can access all of the power of the IBM Watson Platform and build applications using prebuilt services and APIs. This is where you can also initially access IBM Watson Analytics.
- Like the IBM Cloud dashboard, the Watson Analytics dashboard is organized with a title or menu bar across the top of the page then (below the page) you'll find the **Search/Add/Filter/Sort** bar followed by an open space where content panels will appear.
- Under the Watson Analytics menu bar is the **Quick Start Information** bar consisting of larger icons used to organize and provide for quick access to: Explore, Predict, Assemble, Social Media, and Refine.
- In the Watson search bar, you will find the features that allow you to search for, sort, and otherwise filter the content panels/tiles that currently exist within your Watson Analytics account. In the center, perhaps the most important, is the **Add** icon, allowing you to create new Watson assets or add more data to your Watson account.
- All of the Watson Analytics assets that you either previously created or have been granted access to show up in the content panel area as individual content panels/tiles that you can click on, to access and edit/update.
- **Explore** is designed to allow you to use **visualizations** to gain an understanding of the data you are interested in so that you can notice patterns and relationships within that.
- **Predict** delivers insights based on internal modeling in the form of predictions based on the data you provide.
- Another fundamental feature of IBM Watson is **Assemble**. Simply put, you can use this to *group* the results generated from using **Explore** and **Predict**.
- Newer to IBM's Watson is the built-in Social Media capabilities designed to allow discovery of insights based upon data gathered by IBM Watson from keywords and hashtags you choose.
- IBM Watson **Refine** provides the ability to hone, enhance, polish, improve, or even perfect the data you are planning to use in your IBM Watson Analytics project.
- You can add new data to IBM Watson without. The data can be contained in a cloud-based or on-premise database, or simply uploaded to IBM Watson as a simple text file.

Chapter 2 – A Basic Watson Project

In Chapter 2, we elected to use a use case project that analyzed **trip log data** from a driving services company to determine which trip characteristics have a direct effect on a trip's profitability; what type of trip is most profitable, and which are prone to complications. This first, most basic project served to cover the fundamental components present in almost every Watson Analytics project—preparing the reader for the more complex projects presented in remaining chapters.

Key takeaways:

- The key capabilities of Watson Analytics include: automated data discovery, exploration, guided predictive analytics, recommended visualizations, dashboard creation, and visual storytelling.
- Projects start with gaining an understanding of the need or objective (for doing the project). After that, a review of the data fields available in the data is required.
- Projects may also include building a **project data pool** (or a single, secure location of all the data we intend to use) to be the input to our Watson project. The method used to create a data pool varies by project and requirement.
- To add data to Watson Analytics, go to the main or **Welcome** page, click on the + **Add** icon, then select: **Drop file or browse** or **Upload data**.
- Data quality assesses the degree to which a dataset is suitable for analysis. A shorthand representation of this assessment is the data quality score. The score is measured on a scale of 0-100, with 100 representing the highest possible data quality.
- To obtain a high data quality score, clean your data before you import it into Watson Analytics.
- You can use Refine to polish your data. This is sometimes referred to as *tuning* your data. When you refine a dataset in Watson, a new dataset is created that is *related* to your original dataset, but always saved as a *separate version* of the original dataset.
- Sometimes, especially if you are dealing with data completely new to you, you may spend time first exploring your data using Watson Analytics' Explore feature
- Using Watson Predict, Watson Analytics uses these sophisticated algorithms to quickly and efficiently deliver predictions based on your data.

- The predictions include visualizations and text descriptions of the analyses that Watson Analytics runs. You can use the visualizations to see the analyses at a glance and read the text for supporting explanations and statistical details.
- A Watson Analytics prediction is a container for a predictive analysis.
- When the prediction is ready, you can view the results starting with the **Top Predictors** page where you can select a predictor that is interesting and open its visualization.

Chapter 3 – An Automated Supply Chain Scenario

In Chapter 3, our use case project focused on analyzing how effective a supply chain is for a retail department store scenario. The automated supply chain scenario looked to provide insights to an organization's supply chain data and processes, in an attempt to find delivery performance problems.

Key takeaways:

- Although supply chain management has multiple objectives, one of the most fundamental is achieving efficient fulfillment. **Efficient fulfillment** is the process of making inventory readily available to the customer to fulfill demand.
- *Readily Available* must also be accompanied by the most efficient use of cross-chain resources, maintaining minimal inventory levels, incurring little or no waste and permitting the lowest costs overall.
- Supply chain data is not singular in source, in that it is comprised of a variety of informational data points and collections such as accounts payable, accounts receivable, manufacturing data, cost of goods sold, various vendor records, and so on.
- Rather than obtaining a field-by-field description of the data, you can use the Watson Analytics Exploration feature to get to know data.
- Based upon your Watson Analytics subscription level, there are specific limitations to the data and format that can be loaded.
- To initiate an Explore, you click on the Explore image in the upper left of the **Welcome** page. Watson Analytics automatically explores your data and presents its findings as a page of *entry points* or *prompts*.
- To see the answer to a prompt or question, you click on the question and Watson Analytics runs a query and presents the results in an visualization.

- Watson automates the process of having to: think of a question (query), formulate a query based upon the question, execute the query, review resultant data, think of an appropriate visualization type, create the visualization using the query's result, and draw a conclusion.
- As you type, Watson Analytics autofills column names from the data and quickly generates a list of exploration prompts related to the question.
- You can drill into a prompt and IBM Watson Analytics will provide a relevant visualization.
- Obtaining insights from data with Watson Analytics is accomplished with the Predict feature. The steps for creating a prediction are simple. These steps are referred to as a **Prediction Workflow**.
- **A predictor** variable is a variable that can be used to predict the value of another variable.
- When you open a Watson Analytics prediction, the **Top Predictors page** appears. The *spiral visualization* you see shows you the top key drivers, or predictors (in color with other predictors in gray). The closer the predictor is to the center of the spiral, the stronger that predictor is.
- The results of predictions in IBM Watson Analytics are presented as a combination of both *visual* and *text* insights.
- You use the Assemble capability in Watson Analytics to convey analysis and insights. You can use Assemble to assemble Watson assets as well as external files (such as images) into Watson interactive **views**. Views can be either dashboards or stories and can be easily shared with others.
- A Watson Analytics dashboard is a kind of view that helps you to monitor events or activities at a glance by providing key insights and analysis about data on one or more pages or screens. Types of dashboard include single-page, tabbed, and infographic.

Chapter 4 – Healthcare Dialoguing

In this chapter, we covered the concept of a Watsons Analytics cognitive assistance solution which focused on creating a dialog between a healthcare provider and its patients, in an attempt to establish relevant recommendations based upon patient inputs.

Key takeaways:

- Often healthcare data is defined as the data related to a person's medical history including symptoms, diagnoses, procedures, and outcomes. We can also say that the purpose of this healthcare information is to provide useful and meaningful insights so that it can be used properly and effectively to achieve an objective.
- Patient dialoguing can help move from a care giver checking off a patient's symptoms and then applying appropriate treatments to identifying risk and making predictive recommendations.
- Dialoguing data comprises statements made between patient and healthcare providers, including *naturally occurring* narratives shared by patients with their physicians at key decision points along the patient's journey.
- Dialog data characteristics include various types of data, including symptoms, length of discussions, top questions asked, and so on.
- The project reinforced the practice of identifying a (project) goal, determining what data is available for use, and then reviewing and understanding the data before loading that data into Watson Analytics.
- Although dialoguing isn't always saved in a formatted (or at least a consistently formatted) way, it is easiest to consume and use with Watson Analytics, if some time is taken to apply at least some degree of formatting to the data.
- Dialoguing data is often of three types: system-based medical history, automated dialog content, and physician observations.
- Once the data has loaded one approach to getting to know it is to create a prediction on the data, then edit its properties.
- The **Field Properties** page lists every column found in the data down the left of the page. Clicking on a column selects it and allows you to see the name of the column, the label being used for the column, its role, and its measurement level.
- If at some point you are not sure of the next steps to take with your data, you can use Watson Analytics Explore to keep moving forward.
- You can use the Watson Analytics prompts or enter your own. If you select a prompt, across the top of the page there is a band of useful information based upon the current visualization. Visualizations can be drilled into for additional information.
- Interesting observations can be saved for later use. IBM Watson Analytics lets you save these as collected assets.
- Assets can be added to dashboards and stories that you create in Assemble.

- The visualizations collected remain interactive.
- Data quality is the degree to which the data is suitable for analysis.
- Watson Analytics' assessment of the quality of data is a score measured on a scale of 0-100, with 100 representing the highest possible data quality.
- The Watson Analytics Data Quality Report provides graphical and textual information about the data quality of the data analyzed.
- To build a story of your analysis, you use Assemble, available from the Watson Analytics **Welcome** page by clicking on **Assemble**.

Chapter 5 – Social Media Sentiment Analysis

In Chapter 5, we learned about **sentiment analysis** using Watson Analytics' new social media feature to automatically analyze and categorize text posted to social media, in an attempt to determine an audience's feeling about a topic.

Key takeaways:

- Sentiment analysis can often be referred to as **opinion mining** and *IBM Watson Analytics for Social Media* is a relatively new offering in Watson Analytics and can be used for this purpose.
- The workflow in using Watson Analytics for social media is similar to the workflow that should be followed for all other Watson Analytics project types.
- The social media workflow involves: specifying topics, specifying the date range, specifying the types of source, reviewing the suggestions for your topics, and optionally defining themes.
- Depending on which version (or your subscription level) of IBM Watson Analytics for Social Media you are using, the number and type of social media documents that are supported vary.
- To control the volume of documents that is retrieved, you specify topic keywords, context keywords, and exclude keywords.
- To create a social media process, you click **New project**, then on the **Create a new social media project** tab you enter a name for the project, and click on the button labeled **Next.** At that point a new Watson Analytics Social Media project is then created.

- A topic embodies a portion of social media content that you want to retrieve and analyze. To add topics to a social media project, you type it into the **Enter a topic** text area and then click **Add**.

- You can click on any one of the projects topics and create topic keywords, context keywords, and exclusion keywords for that topic.

- As an option, you can also create investigative themes consisting of an attribute or list of attributes on which you want to break down a topic.

- Just like with any data query, it is always a good idea to try and limit the amount of social media data to retrieve and process. In Watson Analytics for Social Media, you can use a date range to accomplish this.

- You can select which language(s) you want to include in your Watson Analytics social media project.

- Watson Analytics for Social Media can collect from a number of media sources and you have the ability to determine which you want to include within your project.

- Once a Watson Analytics project is set up, you create a dataset with the query results by clicking **Create data.** Watson Analytics for Social Media will then provide an estimate of resources the project will consume and allow you to go back or continue. The results are then written to an **Analysis** tab where you can click on **View Analysis** to view the project's results in a variety of ways.

- Watson Analytics for Social Media automatically generates visualizations as part of the project analysis results and you can interact with those visualizations to do things such as filtering.

- Use *Conversations Cluster visualizations* to understand key terms that appear in social media posts about the topics you added as part of your project. This allows you to *identify trends* and shows you facets and insights that you may not have been thinking of back when you were defining your project topics and themes.

- When you click on the **View Analysis** icon, the default view starts with Conversation Clusters already selected for you. At any time, you can click on the selected tab, then click to navigate to any of the project analysis result types grouped under **What**, **Where** and **Who**.

- You can use the Topics visualization to find trends and share of voice for the topics that you defined. To view Topics, you can click on Conversation Clusters and then select **Topics** (as shown here):

- You can use the Sentiment visualization to understand the *tone* of the social media content found during the analysis. Sentiment is broken down by the topics that we specified when defining our project. *Relative sentiment* shows the dispersal of positive, negative, neutral, and ambivalent sentiment. Sentiment terms are words that measure the tone of a mention. Sentiment indicates whether a mention is positive or negative. A mention is categorized as ambivalent when it has the same number of positive and negative sentiment terms. A mention is categorized as neutral when no sentiment terms are detected in it.

- Sentiment terms are words that measure the overall *tone* of a mention. Sentiment indicates whether a mention is positive or negative. Sentiment terms visualization can be used to refine a sentiment analysis dictionary. This page groups terms into two groups: **Top positive** and **Top negative**. A neat feature is the ability for you again to click on a particular term that you may find interesting or most relevant and see its references (shown in the right pane).

- You can use Geography visualization to inspect where social media documents have been posted.
    - Sources and Sites visualization can be used to compare the different sources of topics, then drill-down to see what sites had the most posts.

- The Watson Analytics for Social Media Influential Authors visualization shows influential authors by source type. Influential authors are those in social media who are actively talking about the topics that we are interested in.

- The Watson Analytics for Social Media Author Interests visualization allows you to look a bit closer at the interest of content authors. The visualization starts with the number of authors broken down by topics.

- Watson Analytics for Social Media analyzes text found in social media content in an attempt to determine the *behavior* of the authors. The Behavior visualization shows the number of mentions by authors from defined behavior categories.

- Behavior categories include: authors that are users of a topic, authors that are prospective users of a topic, and authors that are *churners* of a topic.

- The Demographics Visualization analyzes project mentions by gender, marital status, and parental status automatically.

- *Sentiment* specifies whether a mention is positive or negative. IBM Watson Analytics for Social Media provides you with a default dictionary of sentiment terms. A sentiment term can consist of more than one word and is manageable.
- When you use Watson Analytics for Social Media and create a project, a new Social Media dataset is created for you. After the dataset is created, you can find it on the **Data** page in Watson Analytics.

Chapter 6 – Pattern Recognition And Classification

In Chapter 6, we covered the concept of **pattern recognition** and using Watson Analytics to identify *regularities* in data to positionally classify athletes based upon data.

Key takeaways:

- **Pattern recognition** is the identification of patterns and regularities in data based on prior knowledge or the information extracted from the pattern.
- Pattern recognition is considered by some to be a matured but still exciting and fast-developing field, underpinning developments in cognate fields such as computer vision, image processing, text and document analysis, and even neural networks.
- An initial data review is an important step in any project, even if the review is simply a conversation with the data provider about some background and what might be expected to be in the file.
- Rather than performing an Add, Create New, (Explore), you can click on a panel in Watson Analytics to see suggested starting points to help explore the data through questioning. This method is sort of a quick start-version of the Watson Analytics Explore and shows the **Here are some starting points for ...** display.
- The Watson Analytics **coach** can be accessed by clicking on **How to ask a question** (shown in the upper right of the **Here are some starting points for ...** display page).
- The coach provides individual categories of questions, generated based upon the data which can be reviewed and selected from drop-down lists.
- When you have selected one of the questions, you'll see a new set of starting points.

- Under **Select a category**, there is a drop-down list of categories which includes a category named **Understand relationships and identify patterns,** which will show questions intending to help us use relationships in our data to identify patterns that may exist in it.
- Watson Analytics automatically identifies patterns and associations in the data and then lists new, relevant starting points based upon those findings. These starting points are gathered together and displayed on the Watson Analytics **Insight Bar**.
- The **Insight Bar** displays starting points so that they can be easily noticed, selected, and explored, if desired.
- If we click on a data point within a visualization, we are presented with a short menu that allows us to either **Keep** or **Exclude** that data point from the visualization. In addition, if you click on the 3-dot icon in the upper right of the menu, you can then see the extended version of that same menu.
- In addition, you can interact with a visualization using **Create Calculation, Navigate/Compare, Go Up/Down,** and **Show by**.
- A **trend** is the general direction of a data point over a period of time. A **pattern** is a series of data that repeats in a recognizable way.
  You can just *ask Watson* by typing a question starting with *What is the trend?*
- A **prediction** is a container for a predictive analysis and specifies the dataset that is being analyzed. A prediction can also specify field properties that override the field properties in the dataset.
- Each Watson Analytics prediction can have different targets and inputs. After you create a prediction, you then review it to see the output from the analysis.
- Data quality *will* directly affect the ability to reliably predict any outcome. In an attempt to ensure that a prediction is as strong as it can be, Watson Analytics uses a calculated representation of the data. This is known as the **data quality score**.
- The IBM Watson Analytics Data Quality Report provides both graphical and textual information about the quality of the dataset being used (*a*s a whole as well as the individual fields in the data).
- The data quality score can be affected by missing values, constant values, imbalances, influential categories, outliers, and skewness.

Chapter 7 – Retail And Personalized Recommendations

In Chapter 7, we concentrated on the concept of *personalized recommendations* and the use of Watson Analytics to create specialized plans through *conversational* behaviors found within data. The objective was to create an individualized plan based upon a type of user's prior activities and characteristics found within a designated pool of data.

Key takeaways

- A personalized recommendation means to present or offer someone only those options for a particular situation that *have the most probability of being chosen* by that individual.
- Recommendations are characteristically made based on experienced user behavior such as user purchases, page views, clicks, and even items a user has added to a (shopping) cart but perhaps hasn't actually purchased.
- It is common to come across product recommendation engines which utilize Artificial Intelligence to enhance shopping experiences for customers of online stores.
- A product recommendation engine is designed to give product cues to a user that are *visually related* to current product choices.
- It makes sense to use Watson Analytics to analyze user behavior data and then provide recommendations based upon Watson's ability to identify predictors with the highest prediction strength.
- **Predictive strength** measures how well a predictor variable accurately predicts a target. You use predictive strength to compare the various predictors within data and it is presented as a percentage.
- The fundamental statistical test that determines predictive strength depends on the measurement level of the target. For categorical targets, predictive strength is the proportion of correct classifications.
- Watson Analytics project *cadence* involves conducting a brief dialog on the objective(s) of the project then having a high-level *peek* at the actual *raw data* to be used in the project.
- Before loading the data into IBM Watson Analytics, it is sometimes advantageous to perform some data *preparation*—to ensure that all of the analyses we'll perform are as accurate as possible.
- Some data preparation tasks include: removing filters and hidden rows or columns, removing total lines/columns as well as nested lines and columns, and verifying that all columns have names or titles.

- In Watson Analytics **Refine**, it is easy to test data quality column by column.
- To narrow down the data in a file, you can use Refine filters. Once you have added a filter, Watson Analytics adds a *blue line* or *blue dashes* to the column name indicating that the data in that column is filtered. A brief description of the filter also appears on the column name.
- Once you make refinements to a dataset and save it, Watson Analytics will append the word *Refinement* to the end of the original dataset name and the original dataset is not changed in any way.
- IBM Watson Analytics uses questions rather than SQL commands to generate a list of *starting points* that can be used to create visualizations that meet your needs.
- At the bottom of each page of an Exploration, the current page is indicated by a solid circle *icon*. To move to another page, you click a different circle or view all pages at the same time by using the tile icon.
- After performing an exploration, you should have identified the data points within the data that are of interest to your project's objectives and have a reasonable idea of what to create a prediction on and what the best or strongest predictors might be.
- You can create and compare multiple visualizations during an exploration using bar charts, bubble charts, tree maps, and other visualization types, which can be saved and reused with Assemble; you can also the email the visualizations as images, presentations, and Adobe PDF files.
- Project prediction targets are the fields of interest in a prediction and are influenced by other fields in the data. The Watson Analytics Predict capability defines default targets and field properties for you.
- Across the top of the **Top Predictors** page is the summary ribbon of the predictive model generated by Watson Analytics. The summary ribbon includes thumbnail images showing **Targets**—thumbnail lists of the targets defined in the model, **Data Quality (Score)**—measuring the degree in which the data used in the model is appropriate to be utilized for predictive analysis, **Analysis Details**—showing the total number of columns in the data that were considered in the predictive analysis as well as the number of those inputs that could potentially affect the target, **Top Field Associations** giving the result of the analysis, and **Model Highlights** indicating what the predictive target is and proving a brief summary of the model results.
- When you create a new prediction in Watson Analytics, the prediction opens automatically so you can view it. While you are viewing a prediction, you can see a summary of the most important insights in your data and explore specific fields in detail.

- The spiral visualization or the predictive *bullseye* on the **Top Predictors** page shows the top predictors in color, with other found predictors in gray. The closer the predictor is to the center of the spiral or bullseye, the stronger that predictor is.
- You can use the Assemble capability to convey/share the analysis and insights discovered in Predict (and also Explore) by adding them to the collection by clicking the **Collect** icon.
- Using Assemble, you can view collected Assets, drag and drop them onto a template, and then name and save them.

Chapter 8 – Integration for Sales Forecasting

In Chapter 8, we discussed the concept of integrating Watson Analytics with an organization's forecasting system in order to improve an organization's product sales forecasting effectiveness, by gaining a more in-depth knowledge of the available data, as well as identifying new insights to product performances.

Key takeaways:

- Forecasting is the process of making predictions of the future based on past and present data and, perhaps some trend analysis. Typical forecasting methods are Delphi, Scenario, Subjective, and Time-Series.
- To get the data *out* of a planning system and *into* Watson Analytics, there are several options such as using an ETL tool to export data to a comma-delimited (CSV) file. Another option, when using Watson Analytics, is importing data using a supported data connector.
- Although various tools may provide a way to view data by country, it requires the creation of a report (or view) of the IBM Watson Analytics automatically generates a neat, easy-to-comprehend visualization on the data, automatically.
- All Watson Analytics visualizations are dynamic, drillable, and provide out of the box context sensitivity.
- Insights provided by Watson Analytics can be drilled to by clicking on that insight and selecting **+ New Page**. Visualization types can be changed by clicking on the **Visualization Types** icon and choosing from the list of Watson Analytics-supported visualizations. Depending on the visualization type that you choose, the visualization might be empty because of required data items that are undefined for the selected type.

- Visualization types each have their own precise requirements for displaying data correctly. For example, a bar chart requires *one category column* and *one value or measure column*. There is a full list describing each types requirement available within the Watson online documentation if you search for visualization types.

- You can click on the **Visualizations Options** icon in the lower right of the page to make changes to the current visualization, such as labels displaying style and Smooth Lines.

- Although you might not always use Assemble in a Watson Analytics project, you can save views and visualizations that you feel are valuable enough to view or share later.

- Once you save a visualization, you can update or replace the data it is created on without having to update the visualization itself. When you replace the data in a dataset, the predictions, explorations, and views that are based on that dataset are automatically updated. You can add or delete columns and rows or change the existing data.

- To refresh original data, you can do the following: On the **Welcome** page, find the dataset whose data you want to replace, click on it, then click **Replace all data** and select the new or updated dataset. Now, if you reopen a visualization it will reflect the updated data.

Chapter 9 – Anomaly Detection in Banking With AI

Chapter 9 considered the process of **anomaly detection** from an IBM Watson Analytics perspective, walking through an example use case project relative to the banking industry, in which transactions were evaluated to identify potential fraudulent situations.

Key takeaways:

- In data mining, anomaly detection is defined as the identification of items, events, or observations which *do not conform to an expected pattern* in a dataset and are sometimes referred to as a **rare event**. These events raise suspicion and, typically, **anomalous items** will translate to some kind of problem that requires deeper attention and needs to be addressed.

- Anomaly detection is a technique or method used to identify unusual patterns that seem to not conform to what is the or an *anticipated behavior*. You will routinely see anomaly detection techniques used in many areas such as intrusion detection, system health monitoring, and fraud detection.

- Anomalies are generally categorized as **being point** (which is when a single data point is too different from all others), **contextual** (these anomalies are only a problem in specific situations/context), or **collective** (when data as part of a set becomes an issue).

- Anomaly detection enjoys a wide range of use cases relating to the banking industry such as fraud detection, which is typically categorized as corruption, cash, billing, check tampering, skimming, larceny, and financial statement deception.

- As with all projects, using some knowledge as to the definition of the various types of banking fraud, the project starts with a review of a file of transactions looking at transactions outside of what is understood to be *normal*.

- Even when using a tool such as MS Excel, it can be seen that there are many types of bank transaction found within data and each transaction is assigned a **Business Transaction Code** (**BTC**) that identifies the transaction's purpose.

- The project protocol is again to obtain the data, perform an initial review, and then load the file into Watson Analytics so that we can proceed to the next step in the project, which is usually to begin using Watson Analytics Explore.

- As we've seen in earlier chapters of this book, with Explore you can use language and keywords that you feel are most correlated to the objective(s) of the project to create questions that then help explore and visualize the data in your project.

- IBM Watson Analytics uses *worded questions,* not *programming code* or *queries* to generate starting points you can read through and then use to create visualizations that meet your project's requirements. With Watson Analytics, you develop questions rather than a structured query syntax.

- The chapter's project constructed meaningful questions to ask based upon the projects objectives and compared the questions to similarly focused structured queries that you might run on a relational database, yielding results in table format. Another approach considered was performing sorting and filtering within MS Excel. Even with the power of MS Excel, more analysis was required of the data. Even after adding a filter on certain columns, there were no clear insights.

- Conversely, Watson Analytics automatically created visualizations based on the originally constructed questions. These visualizations made it easier to see larger variances in the data.

- Adding additional filters to visualizations make it easy to see suspicious data events, such as amounts found during this period that are much larger than those that can be seen as the *normal* amount for a particular Bank ID.

- Reviewing the details of visualizations can prove that previous visualization highlights are in fact outliers based upon previously established baselines.

- Using different visualization types, you can better reveal outliers and other **red flag** or audit points in the data. Additionally, you can use the **Visualization Content** section to select or unselect specific data points of interest.

- Using a **Grid** type of visualization, we can see data in a table or row and column format, which sometimes makes it easier to see data as you scroll through it in various ways.

- You can always further explore a visualization be clicking on the **Visualization Content** section and add or remove any data column or row.

Suggested next steps

Now that you have reached the end of our journey, don't stop here! The following are just a few resources or ideas that you can use to become more familiar with IBM Watson Analytics.

Packt Publishing books, blogs, and video courses

Founded in 2004 in Birmingham, UK, Packt's mission is to help the world put software to work in new ways, through the delivery of effective learning and information services to IT professionals.

The website is www.packtpub.com and offers a huge selection of materials for purchase at reasonable prices and is well worth checking out.

Learning IBM Watson Analytics

Please feel free to pick up a copy of my preceding book, *Learning IBM Watson Analytics,* which can be found on the previously mentioned Packt Publishing site, as well as `www.amazon.com/Learning-Watson-Analytics-James-Miller/dp/1785880772`. The book is designed to be a detailed introduction to IBM Watson Analytics.

LinkedIn groups

LinkedIn continues to grow and can be mined for all kinds of information. One group that I specifically recommend joining is the IBM Watson Analytics group which is defined as:

"The official IBM Watson Analytics group is for individuals who want to learn more about using Watson Analytics to get answers and insights from their data. Have open conversations, share experiences and ask questions about how Watson Analytics can help you make more confident decisions".

Product documentation

It may be obvious but check out the product online documentation! It is updated regularly.

IBM websites

On a regular basis, visit the IBM Watson Analytics website: www.ibm.com/watson-analytics, as well as the Watson Analytics user community: https://community.watsonanalytics.com. Remember to use your IBM Watson ID!

Experiment

Finally, use the tool! You can start with the free edition and sample data. The more you use the tool, the more you will become comfortable with it!

Summary

In this chapter, we were presented with a chapter-by-chapter summary as well as what we have (hopefully) learned through performing, or at least following along with, each of the use case projects of this book. And finally, we discussed what you can do to continue with the IBM Watson Analytics learning process and start using Watson Analytics with data or use cases that you're interested in.

Good luck!

Other Books You May Enjoy

If you enjoyed this book, you may be interested in these other books by Packt:

Hands-On Natural Language Processing with Python
Rajesh Arumugam, Rajalingappaa Shanmugamani

ISBN: 978-1-78913-949-5

- Implement semantic embedding of words to classify and find entities
- Convert words to vectors by training in order to perform arithmetic operations
- Train a deep learning model to detect classification of tweets and news
- Implement a question-answer model with search and RNN models
- Train models for various text classification datasets using CNN

Natural Language Processing with Python Cookbook
Krishna Bhavsar, Naresh Kumar, Pratap Dangeti

ISBN: 978-1-78728-932-1

- Explore corpus management using internal and external corpora
- Learn WordNet usage and a couple of simple application assignments using WordNet
- Operate on raw text
- Learn to perform tokenization, stemming, lemmatization, and spelling corrections, stop words removals, and more
- Understand regular expressions for pattern matching

Leave a review - let other readers know what you think

Please share your thoughts on this book with others by leaving a review on the site that you bought it from. If you purchased the book from Amazon, please leave us an honest review on this book's Amazon page. This is vital so that other potential readers can see and use your unbiased opinion to make purchasing decisions, we can understand what our customers think about our products, and our authors can see your feedback on the title that they have worked with Packt to create. It will only take a few minutes of your time, but is valuable to other potential customers, our authors, and Packt. Thank you!

Index

V

visualization
  modifying 186, 188

W

Watson Analytics Exploration 228
Watson Analytics Refine feature
  improving 49, 50, 52, 54, 56
  used, for improving data quality score 47
Watson Analytics
  additional filtering 189
  insight bar 184, 186
  item-based calculations 190, 191
  Navigate menu 191
  using 174, 184
  visualization, modifying 186, 188
Watson Blog 16
Watson interface
  about 15
  add 18

content panel area 18
exploring 8, 9
filter 18
IBM Cloud Glossary 14, 15
menu bar 9, 10, 16
quick start information bar 18
search 18
sort 18
Watson dashboard 16
Watson project
  building 70
  data, loading 70
  data, refining 84
  data, reviewing 3, 71, 72, 73, 74, 75, 76, 78, 81, 83, 84
  insights 89, 90
  prediction, creating 84, 85
  predictors 87, 88
Watson prompts 21
Watson Studio 16
wide receiver (WR) position 176, 205

www.ingramcontent.com/pod-product-compliance
Lightning Source LLC
Chambersburg PA
CBHW080621060326

40690CB00021B/4767